GOVERNMENT AUDIT CONSULTING
What it is | What it is for | How to do it

Copyright ©
All rights reserved.
Original text revised according to the new Orthographic Agreement of the Portuguese Language.

Translator: Hugo Crema Borges Marques
Layout - Luiz Cláudio de Melo

1st edition, 2022.

Cataloging in Publication Data (CIP)
Brazilian Book Chamber - CBL (SP, Brazil)

Sant'Anna, Diocesio
  Government Audit Consulting - Volume I.
Diocesio Sant'Anna - Brasília, DF, 2022.
  226 pags.

  ISBN 979-83-57946-91-1

  1. CONSULTING 2. AUDIT CONSULTING
3. GOVERNMENT AUDIT 4. AUDIT
5. GOVERNMENT AUDIT CONSULTING

CDD-636.089

Indexes for systematic catalog:

1. Consulting

Aline Graziele Benitez - Certified Librarian - CRB-1/3129

Diocesio Sant'Anna

Foreword
Cristiane Casagrande
Paulo Gomes

GOVERNMENT AUDIT CONSULTING
What it is | What it is for | How to do it

THANKS

With the completion of this book, many people deserve acknowledgment for their contributions. Even though I will not be able to name all of them, some I cannot fail to mention here.

First of all, I thank Maria Elizabeth Canuto Calais, a great friend and loyal colleague, who since the book's conception has encouraged me and directly contributed to the work's success. Beth, if it weren't for you, this book would still be a dream! Thank you very much for everything! To you my eternal gratitude, respect, and admiration.

To my friend and master Geovani Ferreira de Oliveira, for the long, enriching conversations, which, as always, added value and contributed to the result of the work.

I thank the enthusiastic, encouraging, and dear friend Hânya Pereira Rêgo for the valuable work of revising this work.

A special thanks to the dear and understanding Dr. Rossana Guerra, who found time in her busy schedule to contribute to this work in the most adequate, propositional, and singular way, as always.

To my friend and Professor Kleberson Souza, for the vital advice and relevant contributions on the subject.

I give special thanks to my dear and beloved wife, Cinthia Sant'Anna, for always encouraging me and understanding necessary absences.

Finally, I thank my three angels who are gifts from God, Julio Cesar, Anna Clara, and João Vitor simply because they exist and inspire me to build more.

Foreword

Dear readers,

The topic addressed in this book is of paramount importance for the execution of internal audit activities. All of us auditors know by now that auditing has to add value to organizations, contribute to the improvement of processes to achieve goals, and help governance bodies in their decision-making.

When it comes to auditors developing consulting work, we may find great resistance from them, who claim loss of independence, objectivity, etc. We emphasize that a good practice to be observed is to follow the *International Professional Practices Framework* (IPPF), not to mention that consulting work is already a reality in many organizations and is increasingly widespread among High Administration. Consulting guides recommendations, in a preventative way, before problems occur.

Throughout the following chapters, the author, in a simple way and demystifying this complex theme, combines theory with practice, describing it in a detailed and at the same time accessible manner *"what is, what it is for, and how to do audit consulting"*. Clearly, consulting services must be previously evaluated by the head of internal audit, to identify restrictions that may harm his or her independence in performing the work. He or she may also be aware that the auditors involved in the work must refrain from assuming any management responsibilities.

We reiterate that, with due care, it is extremely salutary to use this concept within internal auditing activities.

We end our considerations with the certainty that this book will be very important for auditors who are planning or implementing consulting work in their audit plans, and also for professionals who want to improve their knowledge on the subject.

Cristiane Casagrande
General Manager of the IIA - Brazil.

Paulo Gomes
General Director of the IIA - Brazil.

Contents

THANKS 5
PREFACE 7
INTRODUCTION 15

CHAPTER 1 20
why do consulting 20

CHAPTER 2 27
what is audit consulting 27
   2.1 Types of consulting 29
      2.1.1 Counsel-type consulting 30
      2.1.2 Advice-type Consulting 35
      2.1.3 Training-type Consulting 38
      2.1.4 Facilitation-type Consulting 39
   2.2 Scope 47
   2.3 Consulting objects 47

CHAPTER 3 53
RELEVANT ISSUES 53
   3.1 How to do Audit Consulting without Compromising
   Independence and Objectivity? 53
      3.1.1 Conflict of interest 58
      3.1.2 Non-existence of norms and guidelines regarding consulting 58
      3.1.3 No understanding of roles and responsibilities 59
      3.1.4 Technical incapability by auditors 60

3.1.5 Lack of support from high administration 60

3.1.6 Inadequate governance structure 61

3.2 Are there other risks related to the consulting process? 62

3.2.1 Risk of not adding value 62

3.2.2 Risk of working in co-management 63

3.3 What is the best organizational setup for providing consulting services? 64

3.4 Can the IA unit provide evaluation services in a process in which it has previously performed consulting services? 69

3.5 Can the auditor provide consulting services on objects for which he was previously responsible? 72

3.6 Is it possible to perform consulting without a request from management? 72

3.7 What are the main differences between the consulting process and the evaluation process? 73

3.8 Must every audit unit perform consulting? 76

3.1 What objects can be submitted to the consulting process? 79

3.1.1 Governance process consulting 80

3.1.2 Risk Management Process Consulting 83

3.1.3 Consulting in the control processes 85

3.2 Which objects should not be submitted to the consulting process? 89

3.2.1 To decide on a concrete case 90

3.2.2 That the management itself can implement independently of the audit 90

3.2.3 That deals with mere normative interpretation 91

3.2.4 That compromises the independence and objectivity of the unit 91

3.2.5 That may cause administrative co-management 91
3.3 How does consulting relate to the IIA's Three-Line Model? 92
3.4 What are the impacts of the new bidding and contracting law on the consulting process? 94
3.5 What are the main steps necessary for the effective implementation of the consulting activity by the IA unit? 97

CHAPTER 4 98
GUIDELINES AND PROCEDURES 98
4.1 Types of standardization 99
   4.1.1 Bylaws 99
   4.1.2 Mission and purpose 100
   4.1.3 Authority and responsibility 101
   4.1.4 Nature and types of consulting services 101
4.1.4 Standards for the practice of internal auditing activities 101
   4.1.5 Procedures Manual or Auditing Manual 103
4.2 Adequate time for standardization of the consulting process .. 105
4.3 Developing consulting work without the complete standardization of the process 106
4.4 Forms of standardization of the consulting process 107
4.5 Appropriate nomenclature of regulatory documents 108

CHAPTER 5 109
Training managers and auditors 109
5.1 Consulting Awareness Training 112
5.2 Team engagement training 114
   5.2.1 Lectures 116
   5.2.2 Workshop 117

  5.2.3 Meetings and debates 117

  5.2.4 Benchmarking 118

  5.2.5 Forums/Congress 119

  5.3 Awareness training for High Administration and managers .. 120

 5.4 Technical training of auditors 122

  5.4.1 Knowledge about the consulting process 122

  5.4.2 Technical knowledge of the consulting object 122

 5.5 Technical training and the annual consulting plan 123

CHAPTER 6 125

CONSULTING FORECASTING AND PLANNING 125

 6.1 Long-term planning 126

 6.2 Work Forecast in the Annual Audit Planning 127

  6.2.1 Consulting request 128

  6.2.2 Application Review 133

  6.2.3 Consulting program 140

CHAPTER 7 160

EXECUTION OF THE CONSULTING WORK 160

 7.1 Execution of counsel-type consulting services 161

  7.1.1 Consulting Techniques 164

 7.2 Execution of advice-type consulting 173

 7.3 Execution of facilitation-type consulting 175

  7.3.1 Meeting facilitation 177

  7.3.2 Facilitation to respond to external control bodies 178

  7.3.3 Facilitation in strategic committees or commissions 178

 7.4 Execution of training-type consulting 179

CHAPTER 8 181
COMMUNICATING RESULTS 181
8.1 Consulting Note 184
8.2 Meeting Minutes 187
8.3 Training Action 187
8.4 Guiding guide, advisory guidance, guiding primer, guiding reference, guiding magazine, and informative guidance. 187
8.5 Consulting Report 188
8.5.1 Results obtained 190
8.5.2 Conclusion 192

CHAPTER 9 197
Monitoring and Evaluation.. 197

CHAPTER 10 199
THE PROCESS OF CHANGE 199
REFERENCES... 203
Appendix a 208
Appendix B 213
1.1 Consulting in the view of the government internal auditor...... 213
1.1.1 Auditor profile 213
1.1.2 Names of the units 214
1.1.3 Positioning in relation to consulting work 215
1.2 Consulting in the view of client managers 219
1.3 Consulting in the view of leaders of the main institutions that bring together professionals in the area of audit and control 220
1.4 Consulting in the view of the main control bodies and other institutes 222
GOVERNMENT AUDIT CONSULTING 225

INTRODUCTION

Have you ever wondered why you have the feeling you can't keep up with the ever-faster transformation of today's world?

Have you, as an internal auditor, ever wondered why we have to constantly change the way we do things?

I have been following some opinion leaders who claim that "we are not going through an age of transformation, but a transformation of an age".

When I first heard this phrase, at first it seemed like just another pun intended to influence those who take words in a simplistic, superficial way. But upon further reflection, I found a lot of meaning in the statement, interpreting it considering the process of change that has occurred in the last decades.

The proof is that we have almost a dozen names suggested by thinkers, scholars, and scientists to name the current age of contemporary society: knowledge age, collaboration age, Chaordic age[1], abundance age, exponential age, post-digital age, the fourth industrial revolution, etc.

The existence of multiple designations for our time confirms how we are most certainly going through a real process of change.

As I write this book, in the middle of 2021, the world is experiencing yet another great transformation - perhaps the greatest of the century - brought about by a worldwide pandemic known as the "New Coronavirus."

---

[1] Chaordic - a system that combines features of chaos and order.

Unlike most pandemics the world has experienced, this one affected not only people's health, but also communications plus work, trade, economic, and religious relationships, and just about every type of relationship known today.

At this point, we may only accurately speculate that the world will never be the same again.

You may be asking yourself: but isn't this book about consulting? Why then are we talking about changing ages, pandemics, and the future of the planet?

Take it easy! Don't give up just yet! We are talking about all this because internal auditing reflects the environment in which it operates. So, as society and relationships change, internal auditing must keep pace with these processes.

For this reason, an auditor is required to go the extra mile every day. Different and updated knowledge about new ways to work is required, such as continuous auditing, artificial intelligence in auditing, predictive auditing, preventive auditing, and even consulting work.

Definitely, working as an auditor is a great challenge nowadays!

In the last 15 years, I have had the opportunity and the privilege of experiencing, in practice, the ups and downs of the profession: enjoying the joys and sorrows, the victories and defeats, arrivals and departures, but always with a lot of dedication and love for the career.

During this period, I have witnessed internal audit units being acknowledged for their relevant services and relevant audit services being relegated to obscurity.

I saw great professional colleagues bid farewell to their units and welcomed the arrival of new, skillful members.

I have witnessed the troubled relationship between audited and internal audit units and have experienced practical examples of a good relationship, respect, admiration, and contribution between them.

Overall, what remained of these experiences was not the difficulty in implementing a change or the lack of interest of auditors or audited units. What remained was the image of those who truly have a burning desire to change the reality of the Public Administration, through relevant audit work, and the incessant struggle of colleagues for information and good practices that allow them to perform their work in a way that effectively adds value to the organization's business.

It is for these auditors and units that I am writing this book. The book aims to discuss all relevant aspects of the consulting audit process and enable effective implementation in the unit.

For over a decade in this profession, I have had the opportunity to work as a manager of important audit units of public authorities. As Chief Audit Executive (CAE), I have contributed to the implementation of audit consulting processes.

I have also participated in congresses, forums, debate groups, courses, and countless discussions on topics related to audit work. In all of these, one recurring theme is consulting during the audit process.

During debates, it was possible to identify multiple attitudes toward this topic: we have those who are against consulting during the audit process; those who are against but don't give reasons for their position; those who are in favor but don't know how to implement it; those who are in favor and know how to implement it; and activists, those in favor who discuss, defend, and contribute to the discussion.

Which type do you identify with?

Regardless of your position, there is nothing wrong with it, because it is just the way you see it, from the knowledge and perceptions you have.

I identify with the last of them. Not only am I in favor of the discussion, but also an audit and consulting activist. As a result, I have become a manager, speaker, trainer, and writer on audit consulting.

In writing this book, my goal is that everyone understands *What Is, What It Is For,* and *How To Do* Audit Consulting so that everyone can understand this important auditing activity.

The book seeks to guide audit units in developing consulting work, from understanding what it is and what it is for, through training, planning, and execution, to communicating results, monitoring, and finally, evaluating the activity.

Thus, it is a truly practical and simplified guide on how to implement internal audit consulting without compromising independence and objectivity.

To meet this book's goal, I conducted a broad survey with auditors, managers, and representatives of the main congregations of auditing professionals, to capture the real perception of these different players in the planning and execution of consulting work by the Internal Auditing (IA) units of the Brazilian Public Administration.

The survey had the participation of 468 auditors and managers from 133 public institutions of the three branches of government, as well as representatives from the main audit professional bodies, such as the National Council for Internal Control (Conaci), the Federal Council of Directors of Internal Control Bodies (Dicon), and the Institute of Internal Auditors (IIA).

The survey revealed, for example, that more than half of the responding auditors (51%) do not feel prepared to perform consulting activities, and only 2% of them responded that their units do not intend to perform consulting work in the coming terms.

The result of this part of the survey motivated me to write this book, because, if only 2% of the respondents stated that their units do not intend to develop consulting activities in the next few years, and if more than half of the respondents do not consider themselves able to develop this type of activity, it is necessary to provide these professionals with relevant information that can help them adequately use this important tool for IA.

The complete survey is shown in Appendix A and its results will be explored throughout the book. All relevant and necessary points for the effective implementation of audit consulting will be addressed and clarified point by point.

This book synthesizes intense and detailed work, initially planned to take a few months, but which lasted more than two years of research, studies, reviews, and debates. This enabled exceptional results that will certainly contribute to the implementation of auditing consulting by multiple Brazilian Public Administration entities.

Excellent reading, everyone!

CHAPTER 1

WHY DO CONSULTING

Considering the existing controversies and the great debate generated around the theme of consulting, I consider it relevant to discuss some preliminary aspects of the subject, such as whether consulting is necessary.

First of all, I register that the question of why or whether we should do consulting work seems strange to me. In fact, I believe that this discussion is already over, it is no longer up to us to define if we should or should not do consulting work. The debate should be based on how to do it without compromising the independence and objectivity of the unit, applying methodologies that best add value.

This is because, in my view, there is no option for internal audits not to perform consulting work. Not doing it is not an option.

For over 20 years, international standards have advocated for the relevance of consulting as an audit activity. The Brazilian Federal Court of Accounts recommends and acknowledges the role of consulting in auditing. Also, the Brazilian Office of the Comptroller General and the National Council of Justice have established guidelines and mechanisms for consulting work in normative documents.

In the survey in the appendix of this book, over 83% of the respondent managers expressed interest in receiving consulting services for their work processes.

Furthermore, over 88% of the auditors stated they believe the audit unit adds value by developing consulting work.

The leaders of the main congregation institutions of professionals in the area of auditing and control of the National Council for Internal Control (Conaci), the Federal Council of Directors of Internal Control Bodies (Dicon), and the Institute of Internal Auditors (IIA) align themselves with the understanding of auditors and managers who are clients of consulting processes. These professional bodies acknowledge the importance of consulting activities for the improvement of governance processes, risk management, and controls in organizations.

For all these reasons, I understand that it is not an option to choose whether to perform consulting work, but rather a good practice, a veritable way to comply with normative provisions and meet the needs of auditors, managers, and society as a whole.

As will be shown throughout the book, it is crucial to mitigate risks when offering consulting work. On the other hand, there may not be sufficient mitigation for the refusal to provide such a service.

> *It is necessary and possible to mitigate the risks of offering consulting work. But there may not be sufficient mitigation for the refusal to provide such a service.*
>
> Diocesio Sant'Anna

The IPPF states that the goal of consulting is to "add value and improve the organization's governance, risk management, and internal controls processes.

But first, it is necessary to define what "adding value" means.

In consulting, adding value means: offering special advice that promotes solutions that effectively contribute to the achievement of the consulting unit's objectives.

According to Decree No. 9,203/2017, which establishes the Governance Policy for the Autarchic and Foundational Federal Public Administration, public value is understood as

> *[...] products and results generated, preserved, or delivered by the activities of an organization that represent effective and useful responses to the needs or demands of public interest and change aspects of society as a whole or of some specific groups identified as legitimate recipients of public goods and services.*

Following this concept, the expression "adding value" is related to the products offered and the results achieved.

According to the Glossary of IPPF International Standards, internal audit activity adds value to the organization (and its stakeholders) when it provides objective and relevant evaluation and contributes to the effectiveness and efficiency of governance, risk management, and internal control processes.

Thus, in order to add value, the IA unit must, in addition to performing an objective and relevant evaluation, contribute to the effectiveness and efficiency of governance, risk management, and internal control processes.

For value to be added, it is not enough to make objective and relevant evaluations: there must be a contribution to the results of operations or processes.

As mentioned in this book's introduction, adding value is the main goal of IA and, in my opinion, one of the main tools to be used to achieve this goal is exactly consulting services.

Adding value has a lot to do with the perception of improvement, and this perception of improvement cannot occur only from the auditor's point of view, but mainly needs to be from the point of view of the manager, the audit client. In this sense, the value added by consulting work is easier for the audited unit to perceive and measure than by an evaluation service.

Take for example: when, during an evaluation service, a non-conformity is found in the risk management process, and a series of recommendations are issued. Management often does not implement these recommendations, either because of a lack of interest, lack of knowledge about how to do it, or simply because they do not understand the relevance. In conclusion, the desired goal is not achieved.

In this case, although the IA unit may have done a good job, it is unlikely that the audited unit will perceive added value in the work delivered.

In a different way, in consulting work - knowing the maturity level of the institution regarding risk management - the audit unit may foment, facilitate, coordinate, guide, train, and directly contribute to the implementation process of risk management in the client institution.

In this example, the consulting client has no doubt whether the work done has added value to the organization's business, since it brought real change to the process, as agreed with the client unit, and considering its interests.

In summary, one of the advantages of the consulting process is the easy perception of the added value, both by the client unit and by the auditing unit itself.

Therefore, a relevant point is that the consulting process makes it possible to improve the maturity of the governance and management of the consulting unit.

I am not saying that the consulting process is more important than the evaluation process: each has its importance within its proposed scope. However, for many audit units in government bodies, the consulting process is paramount for the consolidation of the IA, as well as for the improvement of the governance and management processes of the organization.

Besides the main objective of adding value to the institution's business, there are other aspects of the consulting activity that are also important for the improvement of the IA unit and the organization itself.

Another important objective is to improve the relationship between auditors and audited units.

The truth is that, in general, people do not take very well to negative evaluations of their work. As a consequence, if we only do evaluations and make recommendations, suggestions, or determinations, this can weaken the relationship between the auditor and the audited unit.

Contrarily, consulting differs from this process in that it does not look for non-conformities or inconsistencies. The goal is not to provide assurance.

Consulting work searches for solutions, namely the best way to structure, improve, or develop the object consulted. This process brings the auditor and audited unit closer together, as their objectives converge.

Another relevant objective of consulting is the continuous development of the auditors: in order to develop consulting work, the auditors need to know the object in depth. Moreover, during the work, auditors encounter people, processes, and tools that will make them even more capable, both technically and in their knowledge of the organization in a broader, systemic way.

Finally, there is a goal I believe is crucial to improve the work of auditors and audited units: developing empathy.

It is not unusual to find managers who are unaware of the auditor's work, who believe that their work is limited to identifying errors and failures, and who are unable to visualize the value added by the audit unit's work.

It is also common to find auditors who lack empathy with the audited unit, and who cannot visualize their difficulties and the technicalities of the audited object.

This lack of empathy on both sides may bring serious damage to institutions. It can go as far as fostering enmity among colleagues.

I usually say that every auditor should one day have been a manager, and every manager should have been an auditor. If this were possible, they would be able to put themselves in each other's shoes, improving their interactions and developing a more cooperative relationship.

Consulting work increases empathy: auditors and managers must work together toward the same goal, *i.e.* to find possible solutions to the problems raised. This enhances the knowledge of the activities of both parties and strengthens empathy between those involved.

For all these reasons, I believe that there are many benefits to be gained from consulting. We must focus our efforts on implementing safeguards that allow the activity to be developed in a way that adds value and mitigates the risk of losing the independence and objectivity of the auditing unit.

CHAPTER 2

WHAT IS AUDIT CONSULTING

The IIA's *International Professional Practices Framework* (IPPF) is the world's leading framework for internal auditing. It is responsible for defining principles, guidelines, and standards for the activity.

The IPPF has used the term consulting in the definition of auditing since 1999; *i.e.* for over two decades, the Institute has established that consulting work adds value and improves the operations of organizations.

Thus, the international standards pay significant attention to consulting work, not only in the number of citations, but mainly in establishing definitions and guidelines for this important auditing activity.

According to the IPPF, in full below, consulting services are advisory and related services provided to the client, the nature and scope of which are agreed with the client and are intended to add value and improve the governance, risk management, and controls processes of the organization, without the internal auditor assuming any management responsibility.

> *Consulting services are* **advisory** *and related client service activities, the* **nature and scope** *of which are agreed with the client, are intended to* **add value and improve an organisation's governance, risk management and control processes** *without the internal auditor assuming management responsibility. Examples include counsel, advice, facilitation and training.*
>
> *(Emphasis added)*

| 27

From this definition, it is possible to reach relevant conclusions on the subject.

The first refers to the **nature** of consulting work, which according to the standard is advisory activities and related services. In other words, every consulting activity is by nature advisory.

Thus, evaluation work is of a different nature than consulting.

The nature of evaluation work is to provide assurance, *i.e.*, it aims to reassure stakeholders of a given work that the information of the object and the results of the evaluation can reliably be considered in decision-making processes. To do so, auditors must obtain assurance that the object of the evaluation is free from material distortion caused by error or fraud.

The ISSAI 200, 300, and 400 standards, which deal respectively with the fundamental principles of financial, operational, and compliance auditing, characterize these types of work as assurance work, whether reasonable or limited. In addition, the IPPF itself defines evaluation as an *assurance* activity.

Consultancy, on the other hand, has a **no assurance** nature, that is, its objective is to provide advice rather than assurance.

In summary, the main nature of consulting work is advisory and that of the evaluation activity is assurance.

However, the nature of consulting is directly related to the type of service that will be provided. In this sense, not rarely is the nature of consulting mistaken for its types. The same occurs in evaluation work.

It is common to come across auditing standards that classify evaluation work according to its nature as operational, compliance, or financial. However, this classification does not refer to the nature of the work, but to the type of activity developed. The nature of evaluation work is *assurance*: operational, compliance, and financial are types of work that should not be confused with its nature.

Thus, it is my understanding that the types of consulting are not the same as their nature, and the nature of evaluation is not the same as its types, although there is some correlation between them.

2.1 Types of Consulting

According to the Glossary of IPPF Standards, examples of consulting services include "counsel, advice, facilitation, and training."

In order to facilitate understanding and seeking convergence with the aforementioned standard, I classify consulting services according to the following types:

Chart 1 - Types of Consulting

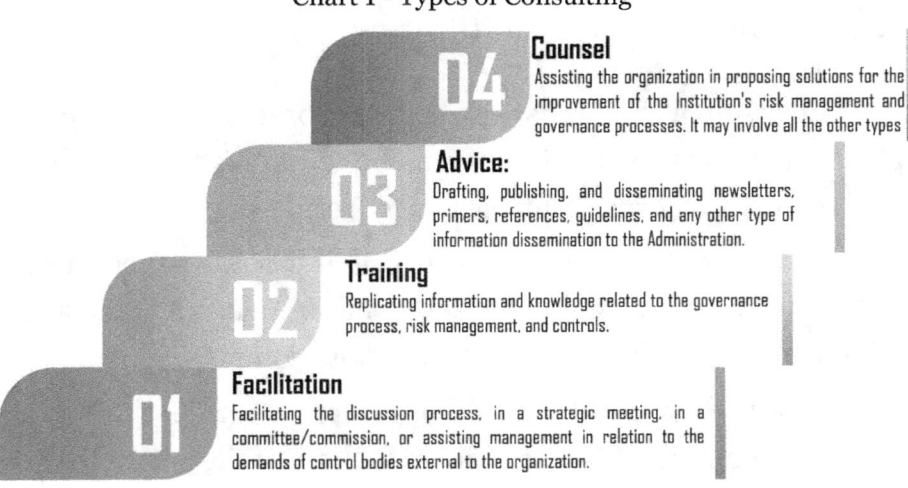

Counsel
Assisting the organization in proposing solutions for the improvement of the Institution's risk management and governance processes. It may involve all the other types

Advice:
Drafting, publishing, and disseminating newsletters, primers, references, guidelines, and any other type of information dissemination to the Administration.

Training
Replicating information and knowledge related to the governance process, risk management, and controls.

Facilitation
Facilitating the discussion process, in a strategic meeting, in a committee/commission, or assisting management in relation to the demands of control bodies external to the organization.

Source: Prepared by the author

In this book, I refer to all of these types of consulting exemplified by the IPPF Standards. Remember that this list of types of consulting is merely an example, and does not exhaustively describe the possible types of consulting. The Standards do not have the power or the intention of doing so.

Also, each organization is free to adopt the types of consulting it deems most appropriate, always considering the objective of the work and the specificities of each institution.

2.1.1 Counsel-type consulting

Counseling means is to assist the organization in proposing solutions for the improvement of the institution's risk management, internal controls, and governance processes.

This is the most challenging type of consulting, because, unlike the others, it is not so clearly and precisely defined, and its scope of execution is broader and more complex.

This is the type of consulting where, as a rule, there is a request from the Administration, in the role of the client, to the IA unit to conduct the work and present the results, which can be delivered in various formats.

In addition, this type of consulting is the closest to the evaluation process and traditional consulting, so more skill and knowledge are required from the auditors. It usually takes longer to develop, and its procedures require a little more formality.

To analyze this, we will cover all topics related to this type of consulting, point by point, so that one can have a clear overview of all aspects related to this type of consulting.

The following is the general workflow of counsel-type consulting:

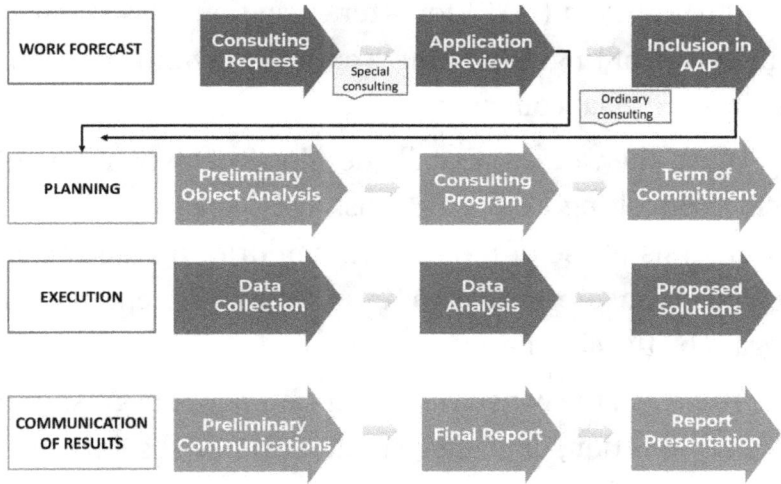

Chart 2 - Counsel-type Consultancy Workflow

Source: Prepared by the author

Initially, we will discuss the items that are part of the workflow above. Here, we do not intend to cover the subject exhaustively as, throughout the book, especially in Chapters 6, 7, and 8, we will deal in detail with all the artifacts of consulting.

Counsel-type consulting starts with a request from the client unit that requires, for example, consulting work to improve the institution's risk management process.

The IA unit evaluates the request and approves it or not, considering the pertinence and adequacy of the request, plus current audit capacity. If approved, it is included in the annual planning, and the team timely develops the work and presents the results.

When the consulting work is previously included in the Annual Audit Plan (AAP) for later execution, it is classified as ordinary consulting. When the work starts without AAP provision, it is a special consulting.

When the work is actually developed, the planning of the specific consulting activity begins. This consists of a preliminary analysis phase of the object, then drafting the consulting program, then presenting to and awaiting acceptance of the program by the client unit.

After this, the consulting execution phase begins. It includes data collection, data analysis, and proposed solutions.

Finally, communication of results is subdivided into preliminary communications, final report, and presentation of the report. Preliminary communications occur during the execution of the consulting between the audited unit and the consulting team, such as meeting minutes, consulting notes, e-mails, dispatches, etc. The final report is the document containing all the results of the work and because of its relevance, in chapter 8 its preparation and presentation to the users of the work will be treated in detail.

At this point, this is the necessary information since each of these items will be detailed in Chapters 7 and 8 of this paper.

It is worth pointing out that other types of consulting can be developed during consulting of the Counsel type. For example, for meetings where the audit unit participates as a facilitator, a booklet explaining the risk management process may be prepared. Additionally, the unit may also be required to conduct educational activities to train managers of the client unit.

Note that the example above contains all listed types of consulting (counsel, advice, facilitation, and training).

This type of consulting is the most complex, but it is the one that produces the most comprehensive and robust results since they directly aid the organization in streamlining its governance processes, risk management, and internal controls.

In Chapter 3, we will further detail and exemplify the subjects that can be audited and those that cannot.

To facilitate understanding, we can understand counsel--type consulting as being residual, that is, if it is not a participation in a meeting, commission, or committee, or facilitation of a discussion process (facilitation), or if there is no transfer of knowledge (training), or if it is not an Audit orientation (advice), we will be facing counsel consulting.

It is worth noting that the term counsel should not be confused with other types of advisory services provided by other units in the organization, such as legal advisory services when a legal opinion on a specific case is requested in order to support proper decision-making.

Therefore, it is not advice on a concrete case, and it is not possible, for example, to request audit counsel on a concrete case related to a specific hiring or retirement process in progress.

An important observation in relation to this type of consulting is that, even when the implementation of the consulted object occurs during the development of the work, it is ideal that a final report be produced to register the purpose of the work: its scope, limitations, and, mainly, achieved results.

An example of this type of work would be consulting to assist management in implementing or improving the organization's risk management process.

In this activity, the audit could initially learn about, study, and assist the organization in developing or updating the mapping of the main institutional processes or macroprocesses.

Second, you could devise knowledge transfer regarding the organization's risk management process (what it is, what it is for, how it can be built, models, roles, responsibilities, etc.).

Third, the audit could help the institution to structure risk management (responsible unit, committees, roles and responsibilities, risk assessment, review, and monitoring)

Fourth, it may help outline good risk management practices that could be adopted by the organization.

The audit could also assist the organization in developing its risk management policy and manual, together with tools for risk assessment, evaluation and treatment, and reporting.

Note that the verb used is TO ASSIST, which means that the responsibility for implementing and perfecting Risk Management lies with management, and the audit is only responsible for assisting and offering counsel that can contribute to the development of the activity.

Note that, in this example, multiple products could be generated: assistance in process mapping knowledge transfers,

Risk Management models, and assistance in developing policies, procedures, and tools, among others.

The example above can be replicated for several consulting objects, always related to governance, risk management, and internal controls, given the objective of each consulting and the specificities of each object.

A potential consulting workflow would include investigating the consulted process (by developing or improving the process mapping), plus evaluating legislation, legal precedent, and especially good practices on the subject.

Transferring knowledge to the client unit enables it to effectively contribute to the implementation of the solution.

Furthermore, the audit would counsel and propose solutions to the organization in the implementation or improvement of the object of the consulting.

Finally, consulting may include the production of a guideline document that will allow the continued improvement of the implemented solution.

If you still have any questions, rest assured! In Chapter 7, I will explain in detail how each type of consulting is executed, with emphasis on counsel-type consulting that, being the most complex, deserves a more detailed analysis so that there are no doubts or difficulties in its implementation.

2.1.2 ADVICE-TYPE CONSULTING

This is the process of elaboration, publication, and dissemination of newsletters, primers, references, guidelines, and any other type of information dissemination by the audit unit to management.

GOVERNMENT AUDIT CONSULTING

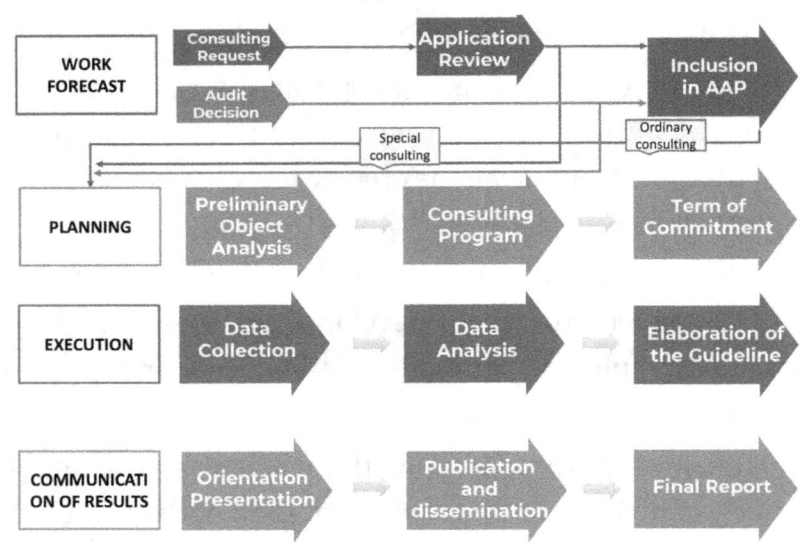

Chart 3 - Advice-type Consulting Workflow

Source: Prepared by the author

In this type of consulting, there is not necessarily a formal request by management. The IA can decide on its own to offer advice based on the experience of the auditors, based on previous evaluation work, and even based on a request from management.

When the forecast is initiated by an audit decision, we may assume that the evaluation of the request occurred prior to the decision of developing the work, and the work is inserted in the AAP for execution in the following year.

When the request for the work comes from management, there is a need for an analysis of the request in the terms already reported for training-type consulting.

The main characteristic of this type of consulting is the drafting, publication, and dissemination of newsletters, primers, references, guidelines, and any other type of informative communication to the Administration. The purpose is to guide them on issues related to governance processes, risk management, and internal controls of the organization.

I recommend that the communication of the results of advice-type consulting be done in the form of a final report. This is important to record results even when several documents have been published.

Many audit units offer this type of consulting and are not even aware of it. A typical example of advice-type consulting is when a routine follow-up (weekly, monthly, bimonthly, annually) of the Court of Auditors' Decisions is compiled and shared with the Administration.

Another example: preparing a primer or other guiding document on specific topics such as Information Security, Risk Management, contracting, or any other subject that fits the organization's governance, risk management, or internal controls.

Note that, in this type of consulting, as a rule, there is no request by the client unit and the result of the work is a document shared with the Administration with relevant information about the governance and management processes of the organization. It may be shared by *e-mail*, access to a platform, in printed or digital form, or any other mechanism that allows access to the document or information produced.

2.1.3 Training-type Consulting

As already discussed in a previous item, IA is usually formed by qualified professionals, and these professionals may work as replicators of information and knowledge related to the governance process, risk management, and internal controls of the organization.

Thus, training-type consulting consists of internal audit members acting as replicators of information and knowledge, related to the topics above.

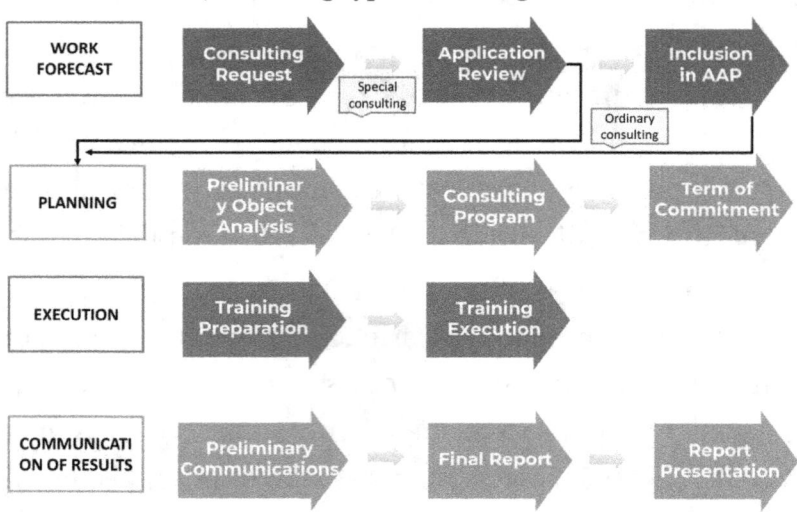

Chart 4 - Training-type Consulting Workflow

Source: Prepared by the author

The forecast of the work begins with a request for a member or team from the IA unit to work as a knowledge replicator in an area or subject matter in an area of expertise.

An important observation related to this type of activity is that consulting is offered by the auditing unit.

Thus, if a given public officer, outside working hours, works as a paid or unpaid instructor in a training activity, we do not have training-type consulting. In this case, the auditor is a training service provider like any other.

In other words, the transfer of knowledge must occur within the consulting process as a product that is an integral part of that service.

Thus, consulting is an activity that is the responsibility of internal auditing, provided by one or several of its members.

It is worth noting that in counsel-, advice-, or facilitation-type consulting, it is possible that the audit unit itself may offer knowledge transfer by internal audit staff. In this case, the training would be offered within an audit of the types specified above.

In Chapter 7, we will deal in detail with this type of consulting, including the requirements for training to be interpreted as a consulting service.

2.1.4 FACILITATION-TYPE CONSULTING

Consulting of this type aims to facilitate a discussion process related to risk management, internal controls, or governance of the institution without the Auditor assuming responsibility on behalf of the Administration.

This type aims to facilitate a discussion process, in a strategic context, such as a committee/commission, and help the Administration deal with inquiries from control bodies external to the organization, *e.g.*: the Brazilian Federal Court of Accounts (TCU), the National Justice Council (CNJ), the Council of Federal Justice (CJF), the Superior Labor Justice Council (CSJT), the Office of the Comptroller General (CGU), the Chamber of Deputies, etc.

For example, when a member of the audit unit participates in a committee, then he or she is performing facilitation-type consulting. When a representative of the audit unit participates in a discussion table on strategic issues of the organization, he or she is performing facilitation-type consulting. This consulting also occurs when a member of the IA unit participates in a strategy meeting, or when IA facilitates a response to an external control body such as a self-evaluation of internal controls, an assessment of the organization's risk management or governance, or any assistance to the organization in responding effectively to an external inquiry.

This is a type of consulting audit units already offer in one way or another, even if it is not classified as consulting and, as a consequence, not registered in their activity reports.

The following is a general flow for facilitation-type consulting:

Chart 5 - Facilitation-type Consulting Workflow

Source: Prepared by the author.

Work forecast begins with a request or invitation for an audit member to facilitate a discussion process in a committee/commission at a strategy meeting or a response to a control body external to the organization, always on matters related to the governance, risk management or internal controls of the institution.

After the request, there must be an evaluation of the request, which consists in checking whether the request or invitation meets all the requirements for acceptance of the work.

The forecast of the work is concluded with the assignment of an internal audit member to the facilitation process.

The final act can be a publication in the Official Gazette, an ordinance, or any other administrative or normative document that assigns a member of an internal audit to some facilitation activity.

If it still seems a little confusing, rest assured, in Chapters 6, 7, and 8 of this work I will deal in detail with all the details of the flow presented above, it is enough, for now, to understand that the request must go through an analysis to verify the possibility or not of accepting the work.

Upon acceptance of the work, the audit team or designated auditor should prepare to offer the facilitation and meet with the group to execute the activity.

The result of this type of consulting, when it is the participation in a meeting or discussion group, is usually formalized by means of meeting minutes. It is also important to state in the minutes that the participation had a consulting nature.

Regarding the participation in commissions or committees, the results can be recorded in the minutes, but they can also generate a final document that registers the accomplishment of the event, when this is the proposed objective.

As for the report, for this type of consulting, for now, it is relevant to know that at least periodically it is necessary to elaborate this document, in order to register all the facilitations carried out in the period.

In Chapter 8 I will describe this form of communication of results in detail.

At this point, you may be asking yourself: can internal auditors participate in a committee or commission of the organization they belong to?

Audit not only can, but should participate in some specific committees or commissions. IA needs to have a seat at the table when important strategic decisions of the organization are being discussed.

> *IA needs to have a seat at the table when important strategic decisions of the organization are being discussed*
>
> Diocesio Sant'Anna

In this regard, the *Internal Audit Capability Model (IA-CM) for the Public Sector*[2] states that for an internal audit to be in compliance with international standards, the head of audit should participate and contribute as appropriate in key committees/management forums.

It also establishes that the head of the audit unit should encourage the involvement of the internal audit team in key organizational committees, whenever appropriate.

Thus, participating in strategic committees related to the governance process, risk management, and controls is essential to the unit: always as a consultant, never with voting power.

To point out committees and commissions that the auditors should not participate in, we mention, for example, a syndication committee, an administrative process committee, and a permanent bidding committee.

In general, IA should not participate in committees or commissions that deal with investigation and punishment or enforcement of procedures or the ones which require voting rights, since voting is a decision, and decisions should be made by the manager and not the counseling unit.

The table below brings together the different types of consulting services with their purpose and examples:

---

[2] Available at: https://www.theiia.org/en/search/?keyword=IA-CM

Chart 6 - Types, objectives, and examples of consulting

TYPE OF CONSULTING	OBJECTIVE	EXAMPLE
FACILITATION	Facilitating a discussion process in a specific committee, commission, meeting, or group dealing with governance, risk management, or internal controls.	Facilitating the completion of the IT Governance Risk Plan. Participating as a consultant to the strategic risk management or governance committee; facilitating a meeting discussion related to governance, risk management, or internal controls. Facilitating an internal controls self-assessment. Facilitating a governance self-assessment Facilitating a risk assessment process.
TRAINING	Acting in a consulting process as an instructor, trainer, or speaker, in an action related to the transfer of knowledge about governance, risk management, or internal controls.	Acting in a consulting as an instructor for knowledge transfer on IT Governance Risk Plan preparation.

ADVICE	Providing guidance, as a rule on its own initiative, to management on issues related to governance, risk management, and controls.	Publishing a Guidance Primer on monitoring the IT Governance Risk Plan; Guidance primer on information security; Guidance primer on price research; weekly, monthly, or annual information on the position of the control bodies on a specific theme; Guidance primer on the implementation of the General Law of Data Protection; Guidance primer on the implementation of the new Law of Tenders and Contracts.
COUNSEL	Advising the Administration on the development, implementation, or improvement of processes related to governance, risk management, and internal controls.	Providing consulting advice for the implementation of the Information Technology Governance Risk Plan; Advisory consulting for improving the organization's risk management; Advisory consulting for implementing the General Law of Data Protection; Advisory consulting for implementing the contract management and inspection process controls; Advisory consulting for improving the hiring process controls; Advisory consulting for implementing the institutional governance policy.

Source: Prepared by the author.

What defines the type of consulting work developed is not the object, but its objective and expected auditors' performance. If it is an occasional performance of specific advice in a meeting, group, commission, or committee, we would have a facilitation. If it involves the transfer of knowledge, it is the training type. If it involves the elaboration of some material that guides the organization, it is the advice type. And counsel is the residual type, a broader work that may even involve one or more of the other types of consulting.

It is important to register that the choice for the appropriate type of consulting to be adopted will always be made by the client unit: the consultant's competence is restricted to suggesting which type he or she thinks is most appropriate.

Thus, it is up to the audited unit to assess, according to the specifics of the particular case, the most appropriate type for the proposed consulting services.

In Chapter 7, we will better discuss this subject, explaining in detail how each type of consulting is executed, with emphasis on the counsel-type consulting, which, being the most complex, deserves better detailing so that there are no doubts or difficulties in its implementation.

2.2 SCOPE

The second conclusion we draw from the definition of consulting is that the nature and **scope** of the work must be agreed in advance with the manager of the client unit. This is because consulting work is done in partnership with the client, aiming to help him implement or improve some process related to risk management, governance, or internal controls.

But first, let's discuss a little further about what is the scope of consulting work.

According to the External Control Vocabulary of the Federal Court of Accounts, the scope is the "Depth and amplitude of the work to achieve the objective of the inspection. It is the delimitation established for the work and is expressed by the objective, the questions, and the procedures, as a whole.

Thus, the scope, in consulting, seeks to outline the field of action of the work. Thus, the extent, depth, time frame, frequency, and any other element necessary and sufficient to direct the execution of the consulting service must be agreed upon with the client, following previously agreed objectives.

In addition to the requirements specified in the paragraph above, the scope also includes the nature and type of consulting service to be performed.

2.3 CONSULTING OBJECTS

In writing this part of the book, I confess that I am surprised at how many discussions it is possible to have with a simple definition of consulting, but at the same time, I am very happy to finally share my thoughts on the understanding of this subject. So now let's talk about the topics of consulting and in which processes it is possible to do consulting work.

According to the IPPF, consulting work should focus on improving the organization's governance, risk management, and internal control processes. In this sense, the Standard limits the topics that should be subject to consulting.

Now you may be thinking: "Wow, how limited is the scope of consulting!

Do not worry at this point! I can assure you that this is not a truth, because the terms governance, risk management, and internal controls are very broad. Let's recall the meaning of these terms according to Decree No. 9,203/2017:

- Risk Management - permanent process established, directed, and monitored by the High Administration, which contemplates the activities of identifying, evaluating, and managing potential events that may affect the organization, aimed at providing reasonable assurance as to the achievement of its objectives;

- Public Governance - a set of leadership, strategy and control mechanisms put into practice to evaluate, direct and monitor management, with a view to conducting public policies and providing services of interest to society; and

- Internal Control - refers to an even broader field, since it encompasses all of the organization's internal control processes. The *Committee of Sponsoring Organizations of the Treadway Commission* (COSO) defines internal control as follows: *"is a process undertaken by the board of directors, all levels of management, and others in the entity, designed to provide reasonable assurance regarding the achievement of objectives."*[3]

Thus, the selection and definition of the object that will be submitted to the consulting process must consider some specific criteria, which will be better described in Chapter 3. The chapter will also define topics that *should not* be subject to consulting.

Moving on, regarding the definition of the object, let us now consider the auditor's responsibility.

Auditors do not have any responsibility whatsoever over the implementation or not of their suggestions by the Administration. Thus, the responsibility to implement or not the advice lies with the Administration, and if it chooses to implement it, it cannot claim in the future that it was due to influence, imposition, or the auditor's decision.

Thus, the advice presented is not binding on the Administration, since the Administration remains responsible for implementing the governance, risk management, and internal control processes of its work and business processes.

If you are still a bit confused, rest assured! In chapter 3, this topic will be discussed in detail, including the precautions that the auditor must take when performing this type of work. For now, it is enough to know that in a consulting process, the auditor does not take any responsibility that belongs to the public manager.

In line with the IPPF Standards, I define audit consulting as advisory and related services where the audit unit works in partnership with the client to assist in implementing solutions to improve the governance, risk management, and control pro-

---

[3] TCU, 2009 *apud* COSO 1992, p. 1.

cesses of the organization, without the internal auditor assuming any management responsibility. Examples include facilitation, training, advice, and counsel services.

> While, as a rule, in an evaluation process, the aim is to guide the institution as to what to do; in consulting, the objective is to help the administration in how to do it, without the auditor assuming any responsibility that is not his own.
>
> Diocesio Sant'Anna

In the same sense and seeking convergence with the IPPF, the Federal Court of Accounts (TCU), in numerous decisions, has consigned its understanding in relation to the importance of consulting services developed by the various internal audit units of the Brazilian government.

Examples of Decisions with recommendations on the subject are:

- Court Decision no. 1.074/2009 - Plenary;
- Court Decision no. 1,171/2017 - Plenary;
- Court Decision no. 814/2018 - Plenary; and
- Court Decision no. 1.745/2020 - Plenary.

By means of Court Decision No. 814/2018 - Plenary, the Federal Court of Accounts (TCU) recommended to the Internal Control Secretariat of the Federal Senate to evaluate the convenience and opportunity to include, in its next annual audit plans, the performance of typical consulting activities.

In Court Decision no. 1,745/2020 - Plenary, that Court of Auditors recommended to the Internal Audit Unit of the Supreme Federal Court the preparation and publication of a

Consulting Manual to guide the execution of internal audit activities in alignment with IPPF 2040 standard.[4]

The Office of the Comptroller General (CGU), on the other hand, has standardized and executed relevant consulting work.

Through the Technical Guidelines for the Government Internal Audit Activity - established by Normative Instruction No. 3, of June 9, 2017 - the Office of the Comptroller General regulated the provision of consulting services by the internal audits of the Federal Executive Branch.

In line with the IPPF Standards, the Guidelines define consulting as:

> [...] advice, counseling and related services, provided as a result of a specific request from the department or body of the Federal Public Administration, whose nature and scope are agreed upon in advance and which are intended to add value and improve governance processes, risk management and the implementation of internal controls in the organization, without the governmental internal auditor assuming any responsibility that belongs to the management of the Audited Unit.

Through Normative Instruction SFC n. 8, of December 6, 2017, it brought the Manual of Technical Guidelines for the Government Internal Audit Activity of the Federal Executive Branch, including the procedures to be adopted when providing services of a consultative nature.

Among the work developed by the CGU, one can mention the consulting services focused on the National Public Security and Social Defense Policy (PNSPDS) and the National Public Security Plan (PNSP). [5]

---
[4] The chief audit executive should establish policy and procedures to guide internal audit activity.
[5] Consulting report available at: https://auditoria.cgu.gov.br/download/13440.pdf.

In the same vein, the National Justice Council (CNJ), through Resolution CNJ no. 309/2020, which approved the Technical Guidelines for the Government Internal Auditing Activities in the Judiciary, regulated the provision of counseling services by the internal audits of the Judiciary.

The Council defines consulting as:

> [...] counseling, advice, training, and related services, the nature, term and scope of which are agreed upon with the requester, which must address strategic management issues, and is intended to add value and improve governance, risk management and internal administrative control processes, without the internal auditor performing any activity that may be considered an Administration act.

Consulting is also defined as a typical internal audit activity in CNJ Resolution 308/2020, which organized the internal audit activities of the Judiciary in the form of a System and created the Permanent Audit Commission.

For all of the above, there is alignment between international standards and the main control bodies with regard to the definition and procedures of consulting.

Considering that the Brazilian control and normative bodies use, as a basis, the definition recommended by the *International Professional Practices Framework* (IPPF), this will also be the basis for my explanation of what is, what it is for, and how to do audit consulting.

CHAPTER 3

RELEVANT ISSUES

As we have seen in the previous chapters, consulting in a more structured way, as a formal activity of internal auditing, is relatively new to the Brazilian Public Administration. Everything new brings uncertainties and questions, and it would be no different with this process.

Because of this, in this chapter, we will address the main issues that must be understood so internal audit units can effectively implement consulting services.

3.1 How to do Audit Consulting without Compromising Independence and Objectivity?

One of the most important points in implementing audit consulting is to mitigate the relevant risk of losing the independence and objectivity of the unit. This is the main argument used by those who oppose consulting by internal audit units.

However, the loss of independence and objectivity when offering consulting services is, in fact, an inherent risk of the activity. It can, however, be mitigated through appropriate controls and safeguards.

Furthermore, a high inherent risk is not unique to the consulting process. Several administrative processes have a high inherent risk, even though they are executed after implementing safeguards to make the residual risk (inherent risk after the implementation of controls) acceptable.

For example, the inherent risk of fraud in a public procurement process may be considered high, however, safeguards (controls) are implemented to mitigate the inherent risk so that the residual risk is acceptable.

The same occurs, for example, in the case of hiring a public officer for the Public Administration: the inherent risk of irregular hiring is high; however, several controls are implemented to make the risk acceptable (mitigated) and make hiring possible.

In summary, many of the processes overseen by the Administration have high inherent risk. Not because of this does the machine stop conducting such processes: safeguards are implemented to allow process execution with acceptable residual risk.

As a result, the statement that one should not perform consulting because the activity has a high risk of loss of independence and objectivity does not seem valid to me. If this argument is valid for consulting, then it should be valid for procurement, hiring staff, paying personnel and suppliers, budgeting, etc.

We well know that none of these processes stop because they have some high residual risk.

Not performing consulting services solely based on the argument of compromising independence and objectivity does not hold water, because when this statement is made, we are talking about inherent risk, and this can be mitigated through the necessary safeguards.

What may be happening is that the internal audit has not implemented the necessary safeguards to mitigate the risk of loss of independence and objectivity.

And I am not saying that the risk of loss of independence and objectivity is not relevant, on the contrary, the risk exists, it is relevant, and it needs to be identified and dealt with. What I am saying is that it is possible to adopt safeguards that mitigate this risk.

But what are these safeguards?

Before listing them, let's clarify what is meant by Independence and Objectivity in internal auditing.

According to IPPF 1100 (2017, p. 3), *internal audit activity* should be *independent* and *internal auditors* should be *objective* when performing their work.

See that independence is related to the auditing activity and objectivity to the internal auditors.

The aforementioned Standard interprets Independence and Objectivity as follows:

Independence is immunity from conditions that threaten the ability of the internal audit activity to conduct internal audit responsibilities in an impartial manner. To achieve the degree of independence necessary to effectively conduct the responsibilities of the internal audit function, the chief audit executive has direct and unrestricted access to High Administration and the Board. This can be achieved through a dual reporting relationship. Threats to independence must be managed at the individual auditor, engagement, functional, and organizational levels.

Also according to IPPF 1110, the chief audit executive should report to a level within the organization that allows the internal audit activity to fulfill its responsibilities. The chief audit executive should confirm with the board, at least annually, the organizational independence of the internal audit activity.

On this topic, the Standard provides the following definition:

> *Organizational independence is effectively achieved when the Chief Audit Executive reports functionally to the board. Examples of functional reporting to the board involve the board:*
> - *Approving the internal audit charter.*
> - *Approving the risk-based internal audit plan.*
> - *Approving the internal audit budget and resource plan.*
> - *Receiving communications from the Chief Audit Executive on the internal audit activity's performance relative to its plan and other matters.*
> - *Approving decisions regarding the appointment and removal of the Chief Audit Executive.*
> - *Approving the remuneration of the Chief Audit Executive.*
> - *Making appropriate inquiries of management and the Chief Audit Executive to determine whether there are inappropriate scope or resource limitations.*

Standard 1110.A1 governs that the internal audit activity must be free from interference in determining the scope of the internal audit, in performing the work, and in reporting results.

See that independence is ensured by the appropriate governance structure of the organization, including the hierarchical placement of the audit unit, so that it is free from interference in **determining the scope of** internal audit activities, in the **execution** and in the **reporting of results**.

In interpreting objectivity, the aforementioned standard (2017, p. 3) rules that:

Objectivity is an unbiased mental attitude that enables internal auditors to perform audit work in a manner that is confident in the outcome of their work and that no compromise of quality is made. Objectivity requires that internal auditors do not subordinate their judgment in audit matters to others. Threats to objectivity must be managed at the individual auditor, engagement, functional, and organizational levels.

Note that for the mentioned IPPF, although objectivity is related to the individuality of each auditor, its management must occur at the individual auditor, engagement, functional, and organizational levels, and the auditor must adopt an impartial and unbiased attitude and avoid any conflicts of interest.

In order to know what safeguards we need to adopt to mitigate the risk of loss of independence and objectivity, it is necessary to know the main causes that can compromise the independence and objectivity of the IA unit, which are:

- conflict of interests;
- non-existence of norms and guidelines;
- no understanding of roles and responsibilities;
- technical incapability of the auditor;
- lack of support from high administration; and
- inadequate governance structure.

It is worth noting that these are not the only causes of loss of independence and objectivity, but they are the main ones, and we will stick to them at this point.

For each of the previous items, necessary safeguards must be established, aiming to prevent the risk from being consummated.

3.1.1 Conflict of interest

In interpreting conflict of interest, IPPF standard 1120 (2017) states that:

> Conflict of interest is a situation in which an internal auditor, who is in a position of trust, has a competing professional or personal interest. Such competing interests can make it difficult to fulfill his or her duties impartially. A conflict of interest exists even if no unethical or improper act results. A conflict of interest can create an appearance of impropriety that can undermine confidence in the internal auditor, the internal audit activity, and the profession. A conflict of interest could impair an individual's ability to perform his or her duties and responsibilities objectively.

Note that objectivity is related to the internal auditor's impartiality.

Thus, before any consulting activity is undertaken, possible conflicts of interest that could compromise the objectivity or independence of the unit must be evaluated.

In addition, IPPF standard 1130.C2 (2017) states that if internal auditors have potential impairments to independence or objectivity with respect to proposed consulting services, the audit work client should be informed before the work is accepted.

3.1.2 Non-existence of norms and guidelines regarding consulting

The lack of guidelines and procedures for consulting may also compromise the independence and objectivity of the unit. This is because, without adequate guidelines and procedures, auditors may be led to act in a manner different from that required for the effective provision of consulting work.

In Chapter 4, the set of standards and guidelines that must be established in order to provide the proper consulting process by the IA will be further clarified.

3.1.3 NO UNDERSTANDING OF ROLES AND RESPONSIBILITIES

To preserve the independence and objectivity of the audit, both auditors and client managers must understand their roles and responsibilities in the work.

Thus, auditors must refrain from performing activities that do not fall within their competence, and managers must take responsibility for implementing or not implementing solutions proposed in a consulting process.

The roles and responsibilities, in addition to being specified in a document, must be widely discussed between the audit team and the client unit, so as not to leave room for interpretation that could potentially compromise the independence and objectivity of the audit unit.

It is worth noting that the objective of consulting is to assist management in implementing solutions that improve the governance, risk management, and controls of the organization, and it is not possible that, in a future evaluation of the process, it is claimed that the audit is responsible for implementing the solution. The implementation of the solution will always be the responsibility of the Administration, and consulting is responsible for advising on possible solutions.

3.1.4 Technical incapability by auditors

The performance of consulting service by professionals not qualified to perform the activity can lead to results that compromise the independence and objectivity of the IA unit. Thus, it is necessary to ensure the proper qualification of those responsible for the consulting process of the unit.

Lack of training can cause auditors to include objects that are not suitable for this type of work; to assume responsibilities that are exclusive to the process manager, or even to obtain a result different from the one previously agreed upon with the client.

Chapter 5 details the types and forms of training to be offered to the auditors, as well as other stakeholders of the consulting process.

3.1.5 Lack of support from high administration

High Administration is responsible for setting the institutional tone as well as fostering and supporting the initiatives that will become part of the institution's culture.

Consulting is a process that generally has members and units of the High Administration as a client, so a lack of support from that instance may cause confusion of responsibilities with the potential to compromise the independence and objectivity of the IA.

High Administration must be the first to understand the role of IA as a provider of consulting work, defending its independent performance in order to better add value to the institution's business.

3.1.6 INADEQUATE GOVERNANCE STRUCTURE

Another relevant cause that may lead to compromising the unit's independence is an inadequate governance structure that does not define and enable a correct internal audit reporting relationship.

An inadequate reporting relationship could impact the determination of scope, execution of work, and communication of audit results.

It is worth recalling that IPPF standard 1110 (2017) prescribes that the chief audit executive should report at a level within the organization that allows the internal audit activity to fulfill its responsibilities, and that independence within the organization is effectively achieved when the chief audit executive reports functionally to the board.

Note that - despite being an important cause that can lead to the loss of independence of the audit unit - its undue subordination does not arise exclusively from the consulting activity, since it can exist even in organizations that do not adopt this work process. However, the more inappropriate this subordination is, the greater the safeguards that should be adopted when offering work of this nature.

Regardless of the type of IA, safeguards are required when developing consulting services to ensure that only the *Chief Audit Executive* (CAE) is responsible for approving consulting work, establishing how it is to be carried out, and how the results are to be reported.

Therefore, the main safeguards to be implemented by the audit in order to mitigate the risk of loss of independence and objectivity are those that attack the causes specified in the paragraphs above:

Key safeguards:
- establishing consulting guidelines and procedures;
- training auditors and managers;
- properly defining roles and responsibilities and clearly communicating them to auditors and managers in the organization;
- managing conflict of interest;
- establishing an adequate governance structure; and
- engaging higher management.

All these mechanisms aim to mitigate the risk of loss of independence and objectivity when providing consulting services and will be explored throughout the book.

3.2 Are there other risks related to the consulting process?

Yes. Besides the risk of loss of independence and objectivity outlined in the previous item, there are two others that I consider relevant in this process; risk of not meeting the previously established objective, not adding value; and risk of acting in co-management

3.2.1 Risk of not adding value

This is the non-achievement of the main objective of consulting work. It is worth noting that the main causes of this risk event refer to the lack of training, the absence of guidelines and standards, and the lack of support from Higher Administration or lack of engagement by managers.

As for the lack of training and standards and guidelines, these have already been addressed in this chapter. Regarding the lack of support from Higher Administration and managers, these are causes related to the lack of guidelines and training that will be further explored in chapters 4 and 5.

The main causes of risk related to the failure to meet the previously established objectives are the lack of guidelines and appropriate procedures to develop the activity and the lack of training of the organization's auditors and managers.

As a result, if auditors and managers are trained, and if guidelines and procedures have been established, everyone involved knows what to do, how to do it, and most importantly, knows what *not to do*, and they do not jeopardize the results of the work or even the independence and objectivity of the unit.

3.2.2 RISK OF WORKING IN CO-MANAGEMENT

Another relevant risk in the consulting process is the possibility of interfering in the Administration's exclusive duties, which we call administrative co-management.

It is a common understanding among control bodies that the IA unit should not work in typical management activities, because, by doing so, it would be working in co-management and compromising the independence and objectivity of the unit.

The National Justice Council (CNJ), through Resolution CNJ no. 308/2020, established, in the sole paragraph of Article 2, that, in view of their main attributions, internal audit units are prohibited from performing typical management activities, and are not allowed to participate in the regular course of administrative processes or to perform practices that constitute management acts.

In the same vein, the Federal Court of Accounts (TCU), in a series of rulings - such as 2,622/2015 - Plenary - has recommended observing the conceptual differences between internal control and internal audit, so as not to assign co-management activities to the internal audit unit.

Thus, the internal audit unit should not perform typical management activities, whether in an evaluation or consulting process.

Thus, whenever the administration requests consulting work, the unit must evaluate whether the object of the consultation is a typical activity of the manager or whether it is related to the improvement of governance processes, risk management, or the organization's controls. Auditors must remember that managers' typical, exclusive duties are those related to the execution and the decision in the specific case, as discussed above.

It is important to remember that in addition to managing the risks of the consulting process, it is necessary to manage the risks of each specific consulting service, according to the specifics of the object.

3.3 WHAT IS THE BEST ORGANIZATIONAL SETUP FOR PROVIDING CONSULTING SERVICES?

The organizational setup refers to the internal division of the auditing unit, for the development of the consulting service.

CHAPTER 3 - RELEVANT ISSUES

Since the way consulting services are provided varies according to the specifics of each IA unit, the pros and cons of the different structures that can be used by internal audits are presented below.

Basically, there are three different ways of setting up consulting work:

1. a specific subunit exclusively performs consulting services and is not responsible for evaluation services;
2. all subunit auditors perform consulting work, and a specific team is appointed for each work to be developed, and finally; or
3. a combination of these two structures.

It is also possible to glimpse the existence of a fourth configuration, which would be a structure by projects, however, due to the recency of this model in Brazilian public administration, I will not address it for now.

Let us examine each of the three in detail.

Table 7 - Structure with Specific Consulting Subunit

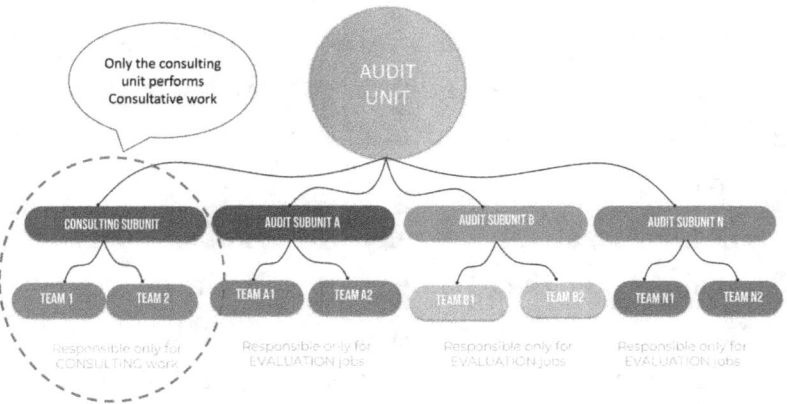

Source: Prepared by the author

A positive point of the creation of a specific unit to perform consulting work is the possibility of this unit specializing in a single activity. This reduces the possibility of conflict of interest, as the professional who performed the counseling will not be responsible for evaluating it in a possible future activity. Another positive point of this setup is related to communication with those involved in the consulting process, especially for clients, which becomes clearer due to the existence of a physical unit responsible exclusively for consulting work.

A negative point of this type of configuration is that it does not allow auditors with extensive experience in relation to risk management, governance, and internal controls to participate in the process if they are not hierarchically linked to the consulting unit.

Another negative point is the fact that there is no possibility of homogeneity of understanding throughout the audit unit, since each team, whether consulting or auditing, carries out the work separately.

The final negative point refers to the impossibility of increased learning for all the members of IA, obtained when conducting consulting work, especially those related to empathy with customers and improvement of personal and professional relationships, as well as the learning obtained by the practice of the activity itself.

Table 8 - Structure without Specific Consulting Subunit

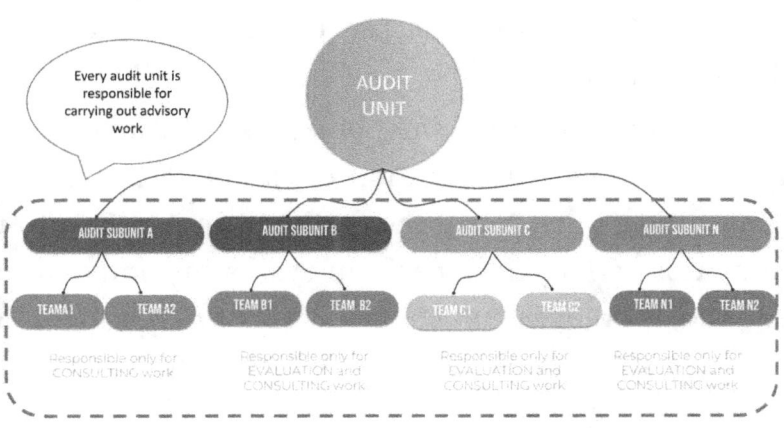

Source: Prepared by the author

As for the consulting services provided by all the auditors without the existence of a specific sub-unit responsible for consulting, a positive point is that all of those who have knowledge related to risk management, governance and controls may contribute to the consulting process.

In addition, this setup offers a plurality of technical expertise due to the possibility of participation of the entire Audit functional body. Finally, there is the possibility of fostering the development of auditors, in view of the practical participation in consulting work together with the unit's clients, which tends to improve the relationship between auditor and audited unit.

On the other hand, a negative point of this setup is the concern regarding the objectivity of the audit, because if it is necessary to perform a future evaluation that covers the result of the consulting service, the participation of the counseling auditors should be avoided.

Still on the negative side, one must consider the difficulty of obtaining specialization of the team in relation to the consulting work, since the auditors, in addition to performing this activity, also perform evaluation and assurance work. And, moreover, not counting with a department dedicated to consulting services may confuse managers as to how consulting works.

Table 9 - Structure without Specific Consulting Subunit

Source: Prepared by the author

Finally, we have a setup that combines the creation of a specific sector responsible for the work, but with the co-participation of auditors working in other sectors of the IA unit, when developing specific consulting work.

In this case, the auditors in the consulting unit are responsible for coordinating the work, however, for each service, a specific team is appointed: it involves the participation of auditors in the consulting subunit, as well as in the evaluation unit, that is, there is the interaction of teams from the entire IA unit, considering the area of knowledge, specialization, and experience of each one.

This setup preserves the positive points of having a specific sector and still guarantees the benefits of participation for all auditors, while mitigating the negative points presented for the two previous types.

A negative point in this type of format is the need to manage the possible reporting to two superiors. This is because if an auditor from the B1 team has been appointed to a consulting team, he or she may have to report to the B1 manager and to the consulting coordinator who belongs to the consulting subunit.

Another concern that remains is related to the need to preserve the objectivity of the auditors, making sure that in the future the whole team responsible for consulting work is not appointed as evaluators of the same process.

3.4 CAN THE IA UNIT PROVIDE EVALUATION SERVICES IN A PROCESS IN WHICH IT HAS PREVIOUSLY PERFORMED CONSULTING SERVICES?

Yes. IPPF standard 1130.A3 (2017) prescribes that internal audit may provide *assurance* services in a process in which it has previously performed consulting services, "provided that the nature of the consulting has not impaired objectivity and with the condition that individual objectivity is managed in the allocation of resources to the work."

Note that, although it is possible for auditing to evaluate the process in which it developed consulting work, the Standard conditions it to verify that objectivity is not compromised by the nature of the service provided and to preserve the auditor's individual objectivity.

The verification regarding the preservation of objectivity by the nature of the service provided consists of evaluating whether the roles and responsibilities have been exercised while respecting all the necessary legal and administrative boundaries when providing consulting services.

At this point, it is relevant to evaluate if the team worked without taking over responsibilities that belong to the administration, respecting all the limits between the consulting role and the exclusive administration duties of the client unit.

With regard to the auditor's individual objectivity, the following safeguards may be adopted:

- adequate staff training;
- guidelines and procedures properly established and communicated;
- roles and responsibilities established and understood by all parties involved in the process;
- proper risk assessment of the consulting work; and
- compliance with the auditor's code of conduct, considering the prohibitions and duties imposed on him.

At the moment, the items specified above will not be detailed, since these make up specific chapters of the book.

In addition to the safeguards already listed, the audit unit must evaluate the possibility of staffing the team responsible for the evaluation with a member who has not worked in the consulting process, and establish a minimum quarantine period for the members of a counseling team to conduct an evaluation on the same object.

Thus, with reference to IPPF standard 1130.A1, internal auditing can establish a minimum period of one, two, or more years for an auditor to evaluate the object on which he or she has worked as a consultant.

It is worth noting that, depending on the specifics of each organization and the specific work, other safeguard mechanisms may be required to preserve the auditor's individual objectivity when performing evaluation activities on the object where he or she worked as a consulting member.

Maintaining the possibility that the object of consulting services may be audited in the future is intended to preserve the independence of the audit unit, which should be free to define its scope of work. However, the audit should not decide to evaluate a specific unit based only on information obtained during the consulting work. The choice of the object must always be based on technical criteria related to risks, materiality, relevance, and criticality of the object, under penalty of the choice being interpreted as partial, leading to a breach of trust, with the potential to inhibit the acceptance of future work by the organization's units.

3.5 Can the auditor provide consulting services on objects for which he was previously responsible?

Yes. Internal auditors may provide consulting services relating to transactions for whose evaluation they have previously been responsible. As established by IPPF standard 1130.C1 (2017), this is due to the conceptual differences in consulting and audit work that will be addressed at the end of this chapter.

3.6 Is it possible to perform consulting without a request from management?

Yes. As already mentioned in the previous chapter, consulting of the *advice* type can be performed without necessarily a formal request by Management. In this type of work, the IA decides, by itself, to offer guidance based on the experience of the auditors in previous evaluation work.

It is worth remembering that, in addition to the examples specified above, the audit unit can work together with High Administration to discuss and promote any of the types of consulting services presented, or even others that the organization has implemented.

3.7 WHAT ARE THE MAIN DIFFERENCES BETWEEN THE CONSULTING PROCESS AND THE EVALUATION PROCESS?

Chart 10 - Differences between consulting and evaluation

CRITERION	EVALUATION (AUDIT *STRICTO SENSU*)	AUDIT CONSULTING
Parties involved	3 parties involved: 1. Responsible for the object; 2. Audit Team; and 3. Users of the work.	2 parties involved: 1. Client of the consulting firm; and 2. Audit Team.
Nature	Offers assurance	Offers advice
Announcement of results	As a rule the results of the evaluation are published.	The consulting itself may not be published, but the result of the work through an act, a decision, or a solution resulting from the consulting activity may be published.
Demand initiation	Exclusive of Internal Audit, it arises from the Internal Audit's risk-based planning.	As a rule, the demand comes from the Administration, but the audit may propose consulting work.

Definition of the nature, objective and scope of the work	Performed by the Internal Audit Unit in the planning phase of the activity.	Defined by the Audit Unit in conjunction with the client unit of the work.
Form of execution	Generally developed only by the auditors, with the participation of the audited unit, when duly called for by the Audit.	Always a partnership between the auditors and the client unit.
Presentation of results	Audit Report. Audit Note.	Consulting Note. Consulting Report. Meeting Minutes. Training. Guidance primer, consultive guidelines, orientation handbook, orientation framework, orientation review, informative guidelines. Other forms depend on the types of consulting and the client's needs.
Recommendations	Mandatory	Discretionary, may or may not compose the result of the work.
Monitoring	Required	Possible when previously agreed upon with the customer unit.
How it adds value	Recommendations issued	Solutions found in partnership with the client unit, trained officers.

Source: Prepared by the author.

CHAPTER 3 - RELEVANT ISSUES

Despite the differences shown in the table above, evaluation and consulting work share common items as specified in the following table:

Chart 11 - Similarities between evaluation and consulting

Common Items	Definition of common items
Ethical Requirements	Integrity, confidentiality; professional proficiency and zeal; and competence.
Objects	Governance, risk management, and control processes of the organization.
Goals	Increasing and protecting the organizational value of public institutions.
Responsible for the work	Public officers as internal auditors.
Quality of work	Planning, procedures, review, supervision, and evaluation of the work.
Operating principles	Technical autonomy and objectivity in performance.

Source: Prepared by the author.

3.8 MUST EVERY AUDIT UNIT PERFORM CONSULTING?

The first challenge is to evaluate whether or not consulting is right for your organization.

A question that I have often answered is: does every IA need to develop consulting work? And the answer is always simple and objective: all IA already performs consulting work, perhaps not in a more structured and formalized way, but certainly performs this type of work under some aspect.

As discussed in the previous chapter, there are various types of consulting: facilitation, training, advice, counseling, and combined. Virtually all internal audit units perform at least one of these types. For example, *advice consulting* may occur when the IA issues some kind of advice to the Administration outside the assessment process.

Another example is *facilitation* when the IA participates in meetings or committees and offers advice that can contribute to the decision of the High Administration.

Now, answer me honestly: does any member of your unit participate in a meeting with High Administration to discuss any aspect of governance, risk management, or internal controls? Or do you serve as a trainer, internal instructor, or training facilitator? Or do you participate in any commission or committee as an advisory member?

If your answer was yes to any of these questions, your unit already does consulting work.

In the IIA Position Statement: The Role of Internal Auditing in Enterprise Risk Management, the IIA states that any work other than *assurance work* should be recognized as consulting work, and the implementation standards for such work should be followed.

However, the great challenge lies in the performance of the advisory type of consulting when requested by the Administration, because it is the most complex type and the closest to traditional consulting.

To state that this type of consulting should or should not be institutionalized, it is necessary to evaluate three important aspects.

Initially, it is essential that the audit unit knows the institution well, and hat it knows exactly how the organization's risk management, governance, and internal control processes work internally, because, in order for this type of consulting to be recommended, it is necessary to identify opportunities for improvement in the work process to be examined, and only by knowing the maturity of these processes is it possible to certify whether there is the possibility, and need, to improve these mechanisms.

Secondly, it is important that High Administration understands this procedure and seeks out this type of activity provided by internal audit, since - unlike in evaluation work, where the auditor decides unilaterally on the planning of a specific activity, in consulting work - the client's interest is indispensable. If there is no such interest, there is no question of consulting work.

It is worth mentioning that, in the survey carried out with the managers of the organizations, 83% of them expressed interest in receiving consulting in their work processes carried out by the IA units of their respective organizations.

So, in general, the interest of the High Administration does not seem to be a relevant problem to be faced by IA. In any case, it is a significant aspect to be evaluated.

Last but not least, it is necessary to evaluate the technical capacity of the internal auditors to develop this type of activity. It is important to verify that the auditing staff has sufficient practical and theoretical knowledge to develop this work.

A significant piece of data, obtained in the aforementioned survey, was that 51% of the auditors declared they did not feel prepared to develop consulting services due to a lack of technical training.

It is essential to clarify that it is up to the consulting team to possess the set of practical and theoretical knowledge necessary to offer consulting work, and it is not required that a single auditor has total mastery of the subject, that is, it is possible that one member knows the consulting process, another has the knowledge and technical skills of the process or activity that will be examined, and a third dominates the practical part.

The theoretical knowledge may already be part of the team, or it may be obtained at the time of the consulting process.

For clarification purposes, practical knowledge is the knowledge obtained through inspection, inspection, survey, management, or any other activity in which the auditor had the opportunity to act directly in the work process that is the object of the consulting.

It is also worth mentioning that not necessarily for all consulting work, practical experience will be indispensable, although it is desirable. There may be work in which, due to its nature and specificity, it is not feasible to form a professional team with practical experience in the subject and, even so, the auditors can contribute with their skills and technical knowledge on the subject.

In summary, the main aspects that can be evaluated to decide whether or not it is necessary to perform consulting activities are:

- knowledge of the organization's governance processes, risk management, and controls by the auditors or team responsible;
- interest in the consulting work from the High Administration; and
- technical training of the auditors who will conduct the work.

3.1 What objects can be submitted to the consulting process?

According to IPPF 2210.C1, the objectives of consulting engagements must address governance, risk management, and control processes to the extent previously agreed with the client.

Thus, the standard already establishes which processes the consulting services offered by the internal audit units should affect. However, in the form presented, these are general processes, which require subdivision in order to define the scope of the consulting work.

3.1.1 Governance Process Consulting

When consulting on the governance process, it is possible to divide it into subprocesses, in order to achieve greater effectiveness in the advisory work. Thus, in this kind of work, it is possible to subdivide it according to the instances of governance. For example:

- Institutional Governance;
- Information Technology Governance;
- Data Governance;
- Procurement Governance;
- Personnel Governance.

Within each instance, other subdivisions are also possible, considering the thematic area. For example:

Institutional Governance
Leadership mechanism
- People and Skills
- Principles and Behaviors
- Organizational Leadership
- Governance System

Strategy mechanism
- Relationship with Stakeholders
- Organizational Strategy
- Cross-organizational alignment

Control mechanism
- Risk management and internal control
- Internal Audit
- Accountability and transparency

Information Technology Governance
- Strategic Alignment
- Value Delivery
- IT Governance Risk Management
- Resource Management
- Performance Measurement

Data Governance
- Data Governance Policy
- Data Architecture
- Business Glossary
- Institutional Capacity
- Communication and encouragement for data management
- Risk management with respect to data governance
- Data Value Management
- Managing the means of data access
- Data related incident management
- LGPD - Brazilian General Data Protection Law
- Open Data
- Transparency

Procurement Governance
- Leadership
- Strategy
- Control
- Plans
- People
- Processes
- Information and Knowledge
- Results

Personnel Governance
- Recruitment and Selection
- Integration
- Job and salary plan
- Gratuified function plan
- Remuneration
- Benefits
- Collective bargaining
- Talent Management
- Performance
- Training
- Workforce
- Quality of life at work
- Succession
- Knowledge management

Remember that the list above is only an example, since it is possible and permitted to provide consulting services in any aspect of governance, with the necessary caveats for each specific job.

3.1.2 RISK MANAGEMENT PROCESS CONSULTING

Another process mentioned by the standard as capable of being offered as a consulting service is the Risk Management Process.

Initially, it should be mentioned that risk management, according to COSO 2013,[6] is the identification and analysis of risks relevant to the achievement of objectives, forming a basis for determining how they should be managed.

In general, the definition of risk management within the Public Administration can be understood as a process to identify, assess, manage, and control potential events or situations, to provide reasonable certainty regarding the achievement of the organization's objectives.

Note that by simply describing the risk management process, you can identify a multitude of possible consulting objects.

Based on the IIA Position Statement: The Role of Internal Auditing in Enterprise Risk Management, the following is an example of what may or may not be subject to consulting:
Chart 12 - The Role of Internal Audit in Enterprise Risk Management

---

[6] Available at: https://www.coso.org/documents/COSO%20McNallyTransition%20Article-Final%20COSO%20Version%20Proof_5-31-13.pdf.

Can be the subject of consulting	Cannot be the object of consulting
Making available to Management the tools and techniques used by internal audit to analyze risks and controls.	Establishing your risk appetite.
Advocating for GRC[7] implementation in the organization, leveraging their expertise in risk and controls management and overall knowledge of the organization.	Enforcing risk management processes.
Providing counseling, facilitating discussion groups (*workshops*), guiding the organization on risk and control, and promoting the development of common language, structure, and understanding.	Ensuring risk management.
Functioning as a central point of risk coordination, monitoring, and reporting.	Making decisions about what responses to risks.
Supporting Management's work in identifying the best way to mitigate a risk.	Implementing risk responses on behalf of the Board.
Guiding Management in responding to risks.	Taking responsibility for risk management.
Facilitating risk identification and assessment.	
Coordinating GRC activities.	
Maintaining and developing the GRC framework.	
Consolidating reporting on risks.	

Source: IIA Position Statement: The Role of Internal Audit in Risk Management, with adaptation.

---

[7] Governance risk and compliance

CHAPTER 3 - RELEVANT ISSUES

Thus, there are many roles that can be played by the internal audit unit in a risk management consulting process. However, the key factor in deciding whether or not a consulting activity can be undertaken is determining whether the internal auditor is assuming any responsibility that should lie with the Administration.

An important recommendation in the aforementioned statement is that where IA is involved in assisting an Administration team in setting up or improving risk management processes, its work planning should include a clear strategy and timeline for moving responsibility for these services to members of the management team.

3.1.3 CONSULTING IN THE CONTROL PROCESSES

Finally, the IPPF specifies that internal control processes can be the subject of consulting.

Internal controls are actions established through policies and procedures that help ensure compliance with the guidelines determined by the Administration to mitigate risks to the achievement of objectives (COSO, 2013).

It comprises the organization plan and all the methods and procedures used by the Administration and conducted by all its officers to safeguard assets, develop efficiency in operations, assess compliance with programs, objectives, goals and budgets, verify the accuracy and fidelity of information, and ensure compliance with the law.

It should be noted that the control process is even broader than the previous two, because the controls are conducted by all agents of the organization and applied at the three levels of the organization - strategic, tactical and operational -, aiming to mitigate the risks that may compromise the achievement of institutional objectives.

Therefore, to define whether or not a control process can be the object of consulting, it is necessary to evaluate at least the following elements:

1. the non-compromising of the unit's independence and objectivity;
2. the relevance of the process;
3. the risks that are mitigated by its improvement;
4. the degree of knowledge of the auditors;
5. the possibility of adjustment of the process by the Administration itself;
6. the effort required to perform the activity;
7. workforce availability; and
8. the High Administration's interest in the work.

Examples of process control consulting are:
- consulting for improvement of the hiring process;
- consulting for improvement of the external phase of the bidding process;

- consulting for the improvement of the management and operationalization process of the budget account;
- consulting for improvement of the cost spreadsheet evaluation process;
- consulting for the improvement of the price research process;
- consulting to improve the organization's procurement planning process;
- consulting for improvement of the preliminary technical studies;
- consulting for the improvement of the asset disposal process;
- consulting for improving the contract management and inspection process;
- consulting for improvement of the fund procurement process;
- consulting for improving the process of agreements and similar adjustments;
- consulting for improvement of socio-environmental management;
- consulting for improvement of the accessibility promotion program;
- consulting for the implementation of the policy of recruitment and selection of public officers and employees;
- consulting for implementing a policy related to talent management;

- consulting for the improvement of institutional transparency mechanisms;
- consulting for the implementation of the accounting records process;
- consulting for implementation of the information security system
- consulting for the improvement of payroll;
- consulting for policy improvement;
- consulting for project improvement;
- consulting for program improvement;
- consulting for planning improvement;
- consulting for improvement of the institutional governance system;
- consulting for improvement of the organization's cost system;
- consulting for clarification of technical questions related to the asset, accounting, budget or financial execution of the organization;
- consulting to clarify technical questions related to the implementation of internal administrative controls in various areas of public management;
- consulting for clarification of technical questions related to bidding procedures and contract execution, exclusively in what concerns procedural, budgetary, financial, and internal control aspects; and

- consulting services to clarify any technical doubts related to administrative procedures concerning processes and documents that, by force of law, are subject to examination by the Internal Audit Unit.

Despite the extensive list, these are just some examples of consulting related to internal controls that can be offered by the IA unit. Of course, everything depends on the reality of each department, because the demands vary from one agency to another and must also be observed in the consulting process.

It is important to note that, when providing consulting services, safeguards should be put in place to mitigate the risk of loss of independence and objectivity of internal audit activity. These mechanisms will be explored throughout the book.

3.2 WHICH OBJECTS SHOULD NOT BE SUBMITTED TO THE CONSULTING PROCESS?

Just as important as the information about which object can be subjected to consulting work, is knowing which processes should not be subjected to such a procedure and under what circumstances.

The following are the main factors that should be considered for the admissibility or not of the consulting object:

- To decide on a concrete case;
- That the Administration itself can implement independently of the audit;
- That concerns mere normative interpretation;
- That compromises the independence and objectivity of the unit; and
- That may cause administrative co-management.

3.2.1 To decide on a concrete case

Decisions regarding administrative acts are exclusive to the Administration of the department or government body. Thus, acts that lead to a decision in the concrete case, be it related to personnel, hiring, budget, or any other segment, should not be the object of consulting, as the unit would be at risk of incurring in administrative co-management.

Thus, it is not possible, for example, to *hire a consultant to evaluate ongoing hiring,* since it is a concrete case. This is true for any process related to personnel, budgeting, and hiring.

In this sense, Article 2 of CNJ Resolution 308/2020 prohibited the participation of auditors in the regular course of administrative proceedings.

3.2.2 That the management itself can implement independently of the audit

The main objective of consulting work is to improve the organization's governance, risk management, and control processes, but internal auditing has neither the capacity nor the intention to replace the manager in the adoption of procedures that ensure the effectiveness of these processes.

Thus, the responsibility for instituting and maintaining them remains with the Administration. The audit is only a collaborator with the potential to contribute to and impact their improvement.

3.2.3 THAT DEALS WITH MERE NORMATIVE INTERPRETATION

Consulting with the objective of merely interpreting regulations does not improve the organization's governance, risk management, and control processes. For this reason, *this type of work can be done by the institution's legal department*, and should not be the object of consulting work developed by internal audit.

3.2.4 THAT COMPROMISES THE INDEPENDENCE AND OBJECTIVITY OF THE UNIT

When evaluating the admission of a consulting request, if it is identified that independence or audit objectivity would be compromised without the possibility of implementing necessary safeguards, the work should be declined by the audit unit.

3.2.5 THAT MAY CAUSE ADMINISTRATIVE CO-MANAGEMENT

Co-management is a term used to identify acts performed by the audit unit that are actually the exclusive duty of the Administration. Examples include:
- participation in a commission of inquiry;
- decision or approval of the object to be contracted;
- handling legal issues provoked by the manager;
- practice of legal advisory activities, which may compromise the unit's independence of action;
- activities or acts that result in the issuing of a commit-

ment, payment authorization, supply, or expenditure of resources;

- filing a process with the indication of authorization or approval of the normative act that results in the assumption of expenses, which must be practiced by the manager; and

- formulation and implementation of policies in the areas of budgetary and financial planning.

Work that may be considered administrative co-management must be refused by the internal audit unit, under penalty of compromising its independence and objectivity.

3.3 How does consulting relate to the IIA's Three-Line Model?

The IIA's Three-Line Model is a simple and effective way to improve the communication of risk management and control by clarifying the roles and responsibilities of institutional governance professionals.

This model initially emerged with the publication, on September 21, 2010, by FERMA and ECIIA, of the *Guidance on the 8th EU Company Law*,[8] as a recommendation of the implementation of the requirements of the law for monitoring the effectiveness of the system of internal controls, internal audit and risk management.

In 2013, the IIA Global (*The Institute of Internal Auditors*) released a Position Statement called: the Three Lines of Defense in Effective Risk Management and Controls.

---

[8] Available at: https://www.iia.nl/SiteFiles/ECIIA%20FERMA%20-2.pdf.

The model was revised in 2020, and is now called "The Three Lines," and no longer "The Three Lines of Defense. The removal of the term "Defense" is justified by the coordination and cooperation that must exist between the lines, and by the role that each one plays, which is not restricted to defense, but includes the creation and protection of value, thus making it pointless to keep the term Defense.

IA plays an important role in this model, not only because it is exclusive to one of the lines or because it offers objective evaluations of the first and second lines, but mainly because it is a fostering and transforming agent of the roles played by the other lines. And this role of fostering and transformation should be exercised by internal audits, mainly through their advisory function, whether it be advice or training.

Thus, in performing its advisory role, auditing can help the organization understand the role of each one in the governance structure, risk management, and internal controls, which ultimately contributes to the understanding of the roles and responsibilities of each one, making it easier to visualize the model mentioned here.

Within the three-lines model, audit consulting ultimately contributes to the independent and objective work of the unit. This is because in many organizations, for various reasons, IA plays the role of the third and second lines simultaneously, and even acts in the first line. In this sense, consulting is an excellent tool to prepare and strengthen the second line, so that the audit is free to act only in that which is its essence, its business, its reason for being.

Thus, by offering advice that improves internal controls, internal audit is contributing to the first line. By contributing to the maturation of risk management, controls, and governance, the first and second lines are strengthened, and by strengthening them, the internal audit function is also strengthened.

3.4 WHAT ARE THE IMPACTS OF THE NEW BIDDING AND CONTRACTING LAW ON THE CONSULTING PROCESS?

In April 2021, the new bidding and contracting law - Law No. 14,133/2021 - was published, establishing general bidding and contracting norms for the Public Administrations in Brazil.

Although it is not the purpose of this book to deal specifically with that law, I would like to make a few comments about some of its provisions and responsibilities that the law has assigned to IA units.

The first comment refers to the inappropriate or improper use of the term internal control body or internal control unit. This is because internal control is not a body or unit, but rather a set of duties and activities that should be exercised by the entire Administration, including internal audit.

As discussed in a previous item, COSO defines internal control as: *"a process by the board of directors, all levels of management, and others in the entity, designed to provide reasonable assurance regarding the achievement of objectives"*.

You see, according to the Committee, everyone is responsible for internal control, not just internal audit or a single, specific organizational unit.

By using this term, the law creates the expectation that it is the control unit that is responsible for control, when, in fact, everyone is responsible to the extent of their responsibilities.

Another point I would like to comment on refers to some attributions defined by law as being the responsibility of internal control or internal audit, but which can only be performed through consulting, under penalty of having their independence and objectivity jeopardized.

Let's see. Paragraph 3 of Article 8 of the law reads:

> *§3 - The rules concerning the performance of the contracting agent and the support team, the operation of the contracting commission, and the performance of contract inspectors and contract managers referred to in this Law will be established by regulation, and the possibility of them relying on the support of the legal advisory and internal control bodies for the performance of the functions essential to the execution of the provisions of this Law must be established.*

See that the law brings the prerogative for the internal regulations to provide for the possibility of internal control to support the contracting officer and the support team.

Here it must be clear that if this support is offered by internal auditing, it should be in the form of independent assessments or consulting and *never* in a concrete case or decision that is the exclusive duty of the Administration, *i.e.*, the support must be offered through a process that preserves the independence and objectivity of auditing.

Note that if the support is given by means of giving an opinion on a specific case, the unit will have its independence and objectivity compromised, since it was not the audit that defined its scope of action, but the regulation or authority that determined what and how it should be carried out by the audit.

Furthermore, the internal audit unit's issuance of an opinion, in this case, equates its activity to that of the organization's legal counsel, since issuing an opinion is a typical activity of legal counsel, not internal auditing.

Audit support may occur, for example, through a process that facilitates the organization's understanding of the most appropriate way to understand and implement the law. Or, through training offered by trained audit staff, or even through advisory counseling, made available by internal audit.

This way, it is fully possible for the audit unit to contribute to the execution of the provisions of the Bidding and Procurement Law, but this contribution must occur without the unit compromising its independence and objectivity, which can be done through different types of consulting services.

Paragraph 3 of article 117 of the law reads as follows

> §3 The contract inspector will be assisted by the Administration's legal advisory and internal control organs, which must settle questions and provide him with relevant information to prevent risks in the contract execution.

Note that the law specifies that the internal control and legal advisory bodies will assist the contract inspector by resolving doubts and offering relevant information to prevent risks in the execution of the contract. In the same sense of what has already been mentioned in the previous paragraphs, I understand that the performance of the legal counsel is different from the performance of the internal audit, *i.e.*, while the former's work is materialized by publishing legal opinions, the latter's consists in counseling, advice, facilitation, and training, without, however, issuing an opinion on a specific case, which may compromise its independence and objectivity.

3.5 What are the main steps necessary for the effective implementation of the consulting activity by the IA unit?

For the effective implementation of a consulting process in the organization, a series of steps is required that will be described below and detailed in the following chapters:

1. establishing guidelines and procedures;
2. training and awareness for managers and auditors;
3. forecasting work and planning the consulting service;
4. executing consulting;
5. communicating results;
6. monitoring and evaluating the consulting service.

CHAPTER 4

GUIDELINES AND PROCEDURES

The necessity of greater and stricter regulation of consulting services has been the subject of longstanding debate among professional auditors, with some advocating a more comprehensive and methodological standardization and others claiming that, since it is a consulting activity, it would not be possible to establish a methodology similar to evaluation services.

In my opinion, standardization is not only possible but also extremely necessary to make the consulting process more effective.

I believe that one of the major causes of risks related to the implementation of consulting by IA is precisely the lack of guidelines and standards establishing how consulting will work in the internal audit environment.

However, there are guidelines, limits, and procedures that need to be established in advance, otherwise, the process will not meet its main objective, which is to add value to the organization's business without compromising the objectivity and independence of the audit unit.

In this chapter, we will study the main types of rules and regulations, as well as what each one of them should contain, with the objective of enabling the effective provision of this type of service by the different internal audit units of the Brazilian government.

CHAPTER 4 - GUIDELINES AND PROCEDURES

4.1 TYPES OF STANDARDIZATION

Initially, it is worth noting that the regulation of consulting is not always exclusive, *i.e.*, even if it is described in the general context of the regulation of audit activities, there is a need for clarification of its rites and attributes. Consulting is different from other audit work. The regulation of internal audit activity precedes the regulation of consulting activity, which is contained in the former, but additional regulation is required.

Basically, there are three types of regulations in which consulting should be included:

1. audit status;
2. standards for auditing practice; and
3. procedures manual.

4.1.1 BYLAWS

The audit charter is a formal document, approved by High Administration, which aims to establish and communicate the IA's mission, purpose, authority and responsibility, and which defines the unit's framework within which it conducts its activities in order to contribute to the achievement of institutional objectives and develop guidelines that make it possible to achieve the Internal Audit function's mission.

Thus, considering that consulting is an important internal auditing activity, the bylaws must define it in all its strategic nuances, including its mission, purpose, nature, and types, as well as the authority and responsibility for performing this type of service.

It is worth pointing out that the audit internal bylaws describe broader and more strategic issues and do not aim to exhaust the matters contained therein, which is why additional rules and regulations are necessary, aiming to achieve the complete standardization of the subject.

4.1.2 MISSION AND PURPOSE

When defining the mission and purpose of internal auditing, the bylaws should make direct mention of the consulting process, in order to describe its organizational relevance as an important mechanism for adding value to the institution's business.

As such, the consulting process must be part of the mission and purpose set out in the audit charter.

The IIA Position Statement defines that the Mission of internal auditing is to enhance and protect organizational value by providing objective, risk-based assessment, advice, and knowledge.

The same document clarifies that the Purpose of internal auditing is to provide independent and objective assessment and consulting services designed to add value and improve the organization's operations.

The Technical Guidelines for the Government Internal Auditing Activity of the Federal Executive Branch states that: the purpose of government internal audit activity is to increase and protect the organizational value of public institutions by providing risk-based evaluation, assessment, and advice.

Thus, when establishing authority and responsibility in the audit charter, it must be ensured that aspects related to consulting services are covered in the specifications.

4.1.3 Authority and responsibility

The bylaws should also establish the authority and responsibility of the auditor with regard to the performance of his or her activities, including the provision of consulting services.

Authority refers to the right and power that the unit has to perform that specific activity.

Responsibility is the duties and obligations inherent to the execution of the activities set forth in the bylaws.

Thus, when establishing authority and responsibility in the audit charter, it must be ensured that aspects related to consulting services are covered in the specifications.

4.1.4 Nature and types of consulting services

The nature and types of consulting services should be identified in advance and included in the unit's internal audit charter.

If there is any doubt or further clarification regarding the nature and types of consulting, Chapter 2 deals with the topics in greater detail.

4.1.4 Standards for the practice of internal auditing activities

In addition to the charter, the audit units must issue or follow standards for the practice of internal auditing activities, which are intended to provide a framework for the execution and promotion of a broad spectrum of value-added internal audit services, including consulting work.

The aim of these standards is also to promote the improvement of organizational processes and operations and to define the fundamental requirements for the professional practice of internal auditing.

Examples of these standards are the IPPFs (International Standards for the Professional Practice of Internal Auditing), the NATs (Auditing Standards of the Federal Court of Accounts), the NAGs (Government Auditing Standards), the Technical Guidelines for the Government Internal Auditing Activity of the Federal Executive Branch, and the Technical Guidelines for the Government Internal Auditing Activities of the Judiciary Branch.

IPPF is the conceptual basis for organizing the statutory disclosures promulgated by *The Institute of Internal Auditors*. They are a set of mandatory, principles-based requirements consisting of: statements of the fundamental requirements for the professional practice of internal auditing and for the evaluation of performance effectiveness that are internationally applicable to organizations and individuals; and interpretations clarifying terms or concepts contained in the Standards.

The IPPF Standards are the main sources for internal auditing, and are even used as a basis for the other internal auditing standards of the Brazilian government.

The NATs define the basic requirements to ensure that the auditors of the Federal Court of Accounts (TCU) are independent, wholesome, impartial, objective, and competent in performing audit work so that they are of high quality, free of suspicion, and worthy of respect and trust by their users and the general public.

The NAGs define the basic principles that should govern the governmental auditing activities of the Brazilian States' Courts of Accounts, providing subsidies to determine the procedures and practices to be used in planning, conducting audits, and preparing reports, and are applicable both to regularity audits - including accounting, budgetary, financial, equity, and legal compliance audits of public accounts - and to those of an operational nature in all its aspects, *i.e.* those concerning economy, effectiveness, efficiency, effectiveness, equity, and environmental aspects.

The Technical Guidelines for Government Internal Auditing in the Federal Executive Branch establishes the fundamental principles, guidelines, and requirements for the professional practice of government internal auditing in the Federal Executive Branch.

Resolution CNJ no. 309/2020 establishes the Technical Guidelines for Governmental Internal Auditing Activities in the Judiciary.

CNJ Resolution 308/2020 organizes the internal audit activities of the Judiciary, in the form of a system, and creates the Permanent Audit Commission.

4.1.5 Procedures Manual or Auditing Manual

The Procedures Manual is the document responsible for establishing the requirements, the methodology for planning, executing, and reporting the results of the consulting activity, and for monitoring and evaluating the results.

This manual can be a separate document or be part of a manual of audit activity procedures. However, in any case, it must contain at least the elements related to planning, execution, communication of results, monitoring, and evaluation of the consulting work.

The manual should contain at least the following information about the consulting process:

1. work request rules:
    a. who can apply;
    b. what can be requested;
    c. when to request;
    d. form of request;
    e. objectives of the request;
    f. provision for the possibility of performing work without a formal request;
2. rules and procedures for application evaluation;
3. procedures for planning;
4. procedures for execution;
5. procedures for communicating the results;
6. procedures for monitoring;
7. procedures for evaluating the work; and
8. rules of work responsibility.

At this point, the items specified above will not be detailed, since each of them makes up a specific chapter in this book and will be defined and detailed in due course, containing all their specificities.

4.2 Adequate time for standardization of the consulting process

A relevant question that I have often answered is: when is the best time to standardize consulting work?

Let's remember that there are three types of regulations that can be involved in the process of consulting standardization: bylaws, rules for practicing the activity, and procedure manuals.

In relation to the audit charter, the consulting activity must be contemplated in the definition of the mission, purpose, authority, responsibility, and nature of the audit work, as specified in sub-item 4.1.1.

In relation to the Auditing Standards, because they are responsible for interpreting and defining relevant aspects of the consulting work, the ideal is that they have already been prepared at the time this type of work is developed.

It is worth noting that, currently, both the Federal Executive Branch and the Judiciary Branch already have specific rules on the subject: IN CGU no. 3/2017 and CNJ Resolution no. 309/2020, respectively.

Regarding the Procedures Manual, because this document is of great importance for the standardization of the services, it is relevant that, when starting a consulting work, this type of document is already available, since the procedures and the specific rules of the consulting process are defined in this manual.

4.3 Developing consulting work without the complete standardization of the process

Despite the importance of the complete standardization of the consulting process, it is possible to start the execution of this kind of work without the complete standardization of the procedure, because the lack of standardization, by itself, does not prevent the development of consulting work.

If the unit considers the provision of this type of service relevant, and the Administration is open to receiving it, it is possible to provide the service by observing some fundamental points.

Personally, I prefer to first try out the process before manualizing, because I have had experiences of creating a manual based only on theory, but, at the moment of execution, verifying that *"in practice, the theory is different"*.

Thus, I prefer to develop a pilot project, *benchmarking* with other departments and institutions that already perform the aforementioned work, experiment, learn from the mistakes and successes, and only then prepare the procedures manual.

This procedure aims to ensure that the normative is more suitable to the reality of the organization. What's more: in a pilot project, the degree of tolerance is a bit higher: errors and difficulties do not carry the same weight as in a mature, formal, professional, and standardized consulting process.

I am not encouraging consulting work at any cost, without the necessary controls and proper risk management in place.

I am only reporting a possibility of gradual implementation, which can even be part of the controls implemented to mitigate some identified risks.

Thus, to start a consulting process without full standardization of the activity, the following conditions are required:

- the IA unit understands the relevance of this type of service;
- managers accept the service that will be provided;
- auditors are knowledgeable about consulting and about the theme that will be addressed during the consulting service;
- a pilot project to provide the service is created;
- *benchmarking* is developed to find the best practices related to the consulting work; and
- the client unit is aware and accepts that this is a pilot project.

It is worth pointing out that the sooner the auditing unit is able to completely standardize the consulting process, the easier it will become to institutionalize it and the more effective the service will be since all those involved will know exactly how they should proceed when performing work of this nature.

4.4 Forms of standardization of the consulting process

The ideal way to regulate auditing activities, whether it is consulting or evaluation, must be done by means of the three documents mentioned above: statute, norms for the practice of the activity, and a procedures manual.

4.5 Appropriate Nomenclature of Regulatory Documents

The name recommended by international standards for the document that defines the mission, purpose, authority, and responsibility is the Audit Charter, however, it is the content, not the form, that really counts.

Thus, if there is a document with the same objectives as the bylaws, dealing with matters related to them, approved by the same competent authority, this document will have the force of a bylaw.

It is worth pointing out that, in the search for convergence with international norms, it is recommended to adopt the appropriate and standardized terms, which in this case is Internal Audit Statute.

With regard to the Standards for the Practice of Internal Auditing, the names may vary according to the organization's understanding.

Do you remember the standards exemplified in item 4.1? Then, each one of them presented a different identification for the document, but they all bring, in essence, the same content.

Regarding the Manual, the important thing is that the document establishes the methodology, procedures, and step-by-step for the provision of consulting work, regardless of whether the name is manual, guide, reference, or any other that the institution deems appropriate.

CHAPTER 5

TRAINING MANAGERS AND AUDITORS

In this chapter we will deal with the main types of consulting training that organizations can implement, which are:

- consulting awareness training;
- team involvement training;
- awareness training for High Administration and managers;
- technical training for auditors; and
- technical training and the annual consulting plan.

This is a relevant part of the implementation of consulting services, because the training of auditors and managers is an important source to mitigate the risk of losing audit independence and objectivity.

Before I talk about the training required for auditors and managers, I would like to make a few comments about the desirable and essential skills of auditors when providing consulting services.

Personally, I do not believe you need superpowers to provide effective consulting services. Just as in an evaluation, I believe that the consulting process can be somehow disciplined and systematized, and this makes it replicable, and repeatable, *i.e.*, the systematization simplifies the process, which facilitates its execution.

However, there are some characteristics that are desirable of auditors who provide consulting services and others that are essential.

The first of the desirable skills is what I call "government entrepreneurship," which can be defined as the desire to do things differently, to add value, to contribute to your work, your agency, and your country. In an audit unit, we increasingly need "entrepreneurs," auditors with negotiation skills, who are leaders and rejoice in achievements, and who are constantly looking for progress and development.

Another desirable skill for consulting auditors is the capacity for simplification. This is a characteristic that helps in the systematization of any process, that is, it is to look at a project, an activity, a product or a task and have the ability to see simplicity in it. It is a procedural objectivity.

Still in the field of desirable skill, I list thinking outside the box, which means evaluating possibilities. It means not just accepting the obvious, it means believing that there must be a different way to design a product or process. Thinking outside the box led to the creation of the iPhone, the airplane, the light bulb, fire, the wheel... This skill will help the auditor not only to perform consulting, but will allow him to do it differently, to do it better, to truly add value to the process.

In relation to the essential skills, the first to be listed is what I call the positive and true intention to contribute. I usually say that before the auditor says "we are here to help," it is necessary to believe this, because, otherwise, it will not be possible to obtain true acceptance from the client of the work. In a consulting process, there should be no owner of the truth, but rather the determination and willingness to find the best possible answer to solve the problem.

Still talking about essential skills, I mention proactivity, which is the need for the auditor to work on his own, seek answers, and identify problems without necessarily having an external charge.

It is also necessary to act with diplomacy, which is the ability to communicate directly, listen actively, have political acumen, and sensitivity to understand the culture of the organization and how it does business.

Another essential attribute of the consulting auditor is trust. Never break the trust that the client manager has placed in the audit. Thus, one must seek to uphold established agreements, operate with integrity, and be determined to sustain credibility with the client managers of the work.

The consulting auditor must also exercise empathy, which means putting himself in the other's shoes, understanding the point of view of each stakeholder, and being attentive to their needs.

Last, but not least, comes leadership, which is the ability to set the tone, and the direction, and keep the team united and moving in the same direction, which in a consulting job is to find and propose the best solution for the consulted object.

I reproduce below a summary of the attributes that I believe are essential or desirable of auditors in consulting work.

Chart 13 - Essential or desirable skills for auditors

TYPE OF SKILL	SKILL
Desirable	Government Entrepreneurship
Desirable	Simplification
Desirable	Thinking outside the box
Essential	Positive and True Intention
Essential	Proactivity
Essential	Diplomacy
Essential	Trust
Essential	Empathy
Essential	Leadership

Source: Prepared by the author.

5.1 CONSULTING AWARENESS TRAINING

Training employees in such a way as to prepare them to perform their duties is a great challenge faced by all institutions, public or private, regardless of the institution or line of business.

The lack of properly trained professionals is a major hurdle that, when not overcome, can lead to performance problems or even the failure to effectively meet the agreed-upon objective.

This would be no different with auditing professionals, who, in addition to evaluation work, are also responsible for performing consulting services, aiming to improve the organization's governance, risk management, and control processes.

In the survey of auditors from the three branches of public administration, they were asked whether they felt prepared to do consulting work and, if not, why not.

Among those who answered negatively to the question, 35% said that the lack of training is one of the reasons why they do not feel able to perform this activity.

In the same sense, 24% of the managers of the organizations who responded that they believe that the audit units are not able to perform consulting work cited, as one of the reasons, the lack of training of the auditors.

Thus, from both the auditors' and managers' perspectives, the lack of training is the main obstacle to be addressed so that the IA unit and its auditors are able to provide advisory services.

It is also worth remembering that when we dealt with risk management in the consulting process, in Chapter 3, we mentioned that the lack of training is one of the possible causes of risk factors such as compromising the objectivity and independence of the unit, the achievement of the desired objective, and the possibility of improper action by the internal audit unit.

It must be emphasized that the training cannot be restricted to the role and responsibilities of the auditor, but must also include the qualification of the process managers, so that they can understand, in a broad way, the whole mechanism of the consulting service at hand.

In this chapter, we will address the main points related to the training of auditors and managers, in order to enable the effective provision of consulting work by the IA unit.

5.2 TEAM ENGAGEMENT TRAINING

For the consulting work to be offered effectively to the organization, it is essential that the entire auditing unit be involved, including auditors, managers of the unit itself, and other employees who contribute to the audit.

It is worth noting that even if auditors are offered fair and adequate training on the consulting process, the involvement will be heterogeneous, *i.e.* some employees will be fully engaged, others only committed, and there will be those who are neutral and those who are extremely opposed to any kind of implementation.

The most desired behavior within any audit activity is *engagement*.

Engagement refers to the act of participating voluntarily in some work or activity; it is doing of one's own free will what needs to be done. These engaged professionals will be the ambassadors of the process, who will act to defend and promote the implementation of the consulting work in the four corners of the organization.

The second type of relationship desired is *commitment*, which refers to the act of committing oneself to something or someone. The committed employee also does what needs to be done, but does it out of obligation, out of commitment to the boss, to the institution, or to the process.

What changes in relation to engagement is exactly the motivation to do the work. The committed person will also help the unit in the implementation and execution of the consulting work because of the commitment previously assumed, that is, commitment is to do what needs to be done out of necessity, whereas engagement is to do what is necessary of one's own free will.

Neutrals neither help nor hinder the process. In any case, it is necessary to train them, because their participation may be necessary in specific consulting work and can also contribute to their commitment and perhaps even to their engagement regarding the development of consulting by the IA unit.

Thus, for the proper implementation of the consulting process, it is necessary to offer training that provides a broader and more general set of information about the consulting process, and should address: what is, what it is for, its importance, positive points, main risks and mitigation mechanisms, types, forms of execution, etc.

Therefore, this type of training must bring clarity about the process, because there is no way to provide a good counseling service without being clear about what it is, what it is for, and how it should be done.

It is also necessary to encourage the participation of the employees in the decision making process, allowing everyone to contribute in some way, either by providing information and suggestions or by acting directly in the preparation of newsletters, norms, and tools on the subject.

The main types of training that can be adopted in order to get auditors involved are: lectures, *workshops*, *benchmarking*, thematic forums/congresses, discussion meetings, and others.

It is worth mentioning that the involvement of everyone in IA in these events can be a great ally for the engagement of all and the mitigation of eventual resistance, because they usually come from ignorance and prejudice about the implementation of consulting.

5.2.1 LECTURES

A lecture is an event in which general information is presented in a direct, pleasant, and casual way, promoting interaction with the public, by means of questions and other forms of participation.

Lectures must be given preferably by a professional with practical experience in the subject, who knows the main benefits of consulting and the importance of its implementation according to the reality of the moment of the units. Especially, this person must discuss the main risks and the ways to mitigate them, to the point of making them acceptable.

You may ask yourself: but is a lecture a good form of training to generate engagement? The answer is: it depends. But it can be excellent training.

It was during a lecture that I heard for the first time about audit consulting. Despite the generic approach and the short time of the presentation, this information generated in me a mixture of curiosity and excitement, so that I became a scholar, an enthusiast and, some say, an expert on the subject.

In this way, I am fully engaged, taking a lecture as my starting point. And the best thing is: with my publications, lectures, and training sessions, I have already encouraged a lot of auditors to get involved and contribute to the development of internal audit.

Although this type of action almost always addresses the topic in a broader and more generic way, it can bring good *insights* to the unit that wants to implement consulting.

For all these reasons, a lecture conducted by a qualified professional is an excellent way to provide initial consulting training and generate internal auditor engagement.

5.2.2 WORKSHOP

A workshop is an event where participants seek to learn and improve techniques in a particular subject through explanations by instructors and hands-on activities.

This type of development is ideal for working on practical situations and exercising both IA's and the Administration's views on consulting.

It is also ideal for generating auditor engagement since it is a workshop, where participants are encouraged to interact and contribute to the theme through hands-on activities, knowledge sharing, and experience exchange.

5.2.3 MEETINGS AND DEBATES

Another way to boost auditor engagement is through periodic meetings held with the entire staff to discuss and debate a certain theme.

In this type of meeting, the CAE (*Chief Audit Executive*) may speak about his views on consulting or pick a member of the group to technically conduct the meeting and bring up specific points for discussion.

The important thing in this type of event is to enable everyone to participate in the debate. The CAE or his appointed office should act as mediators.

It is important to know that the purpose of this type of activity is not to create an ideological discussion for or against the consulting process, but rather to allow everyone to contribute and find appropriate solutions.

Thus, in this type of meeting, for example, the following topics can be addressed:

- discussing the positive points of this type of service;
- raising the risks inherent in the consulting process;
- discussing the controls required to mitigate these risks;
- identifying ways to make the High Administration aware of the consulting process;
- discussing the process of surveying and treating risks in the consulting process;
- establishing criteria for creating the consulting universe;
- establishing criteria for the selection of consulting objects;
- discussing points relevant to the standardization of the process; and
- discussing lessons learned from previous consulting services.

5.2.4 BENCHMARKING

According to the Glossary of External Control Terms, *benchmarking* is:

> *[...] a technique aimed at identifying and implementing good management practices. Its purpose is to determine, through comparisons of performance and best practices, whether it is possible to improve the work done in an organization, and*

may help in identifying opportunities to improve efficiency and provide savings. (TCU, 2000)

For our object of study, *benchmarking* consists in evaluating the effective implementation of the consulting process by other public administration agencies or entities, with the aim of adopting the best practices evaluated.

Benchmarking is an essential tool in public administration, because every resource spent, regardless of the institution, comes from a public budget.

Thus, if a process or system has already been developed, there is no reason to incur a new expense for the same purpose. In this case, it is much simpler and more efficient to adapt what already exists and works to the reality of each organization. Through benchmarking you can develop your actions based on the successes and mistakes identified by the body or unit being evaluated, generating much better results for the process or system to be implemented.

5.2.5 FORUMS/CONGRESS

Another excellent way to foster engagement is through employee participation in forums and conferences.

I have attended a multitude of forums and congresses that are worth much more than many renowned training courses. For audit consulting purposes, we must check the thematic correlation between the event to the desired subject.

Have you, reader, ever heard of the saying "domestic saints cannot work miracles"? Well, this is often true.

It is not unusual to find colleagues, and auditors, saying that they tirelessly guide their auditors on a subject and get no results, and then, suddenly, one of these professionals attends an external event and comes back totally excited, engaged, and wanting to change the world.

So the CAE wonders: what did this employee hear at this event? Actually, nothing much different: just that someone with an outside perspective reported what is often said, and then the officer understands.

Once I was invited to give a lecture in a renowned Forum, which took place in Brasilia. I arrived at the event and gave the lecture, which ended successfully. After the closing, in conversation with the head of an auditing unit, I noticed that he was smiling, apparently very satisfied. I asked him the reason for his joy and he answered: "today you said everything that I have been saying day after day, but now I know that they understood, because they heard it from an outsider, from a new point of view."

Sometime later, on another occasion, I met with this friend and had the satisfaction of knowing that the perspectives had changed a lot in that unit, regarding this matter. "They finally understood what we had been discussing for some time," said the head of that audit unit.

5.3 Awareness training for High Administration and Managers

Besides seeking the involvement of the auditors with the consulting process, it is relevant to raise awareness among the High Administration and managers who are potential clients of this type of service.

Since consulting is a service that, as a rule, requires the client to request the work, it is very important that the entire organization understands the main aspects related to consulting.

The CAE plays a relevant role in this awareness process, because it is through the head of the audit that the High Administration or the Board learns about this subject.

Thus, the CAE must have a previously established strategy, aiming to take advantage of opportunities with the High Administration to discuss and promote the importance of this type of work, offered by the internal audit unit.

In addition to the constant advocacy of consulting by their boss at every opportunity, auditors engaged with the process should act as ambassadors for the IA unit, advertising the role of the audit and the importance of the consulting.

In this awareness-raising initiative, it is not possible to use long-duration training, considering the difficulty of the managers' schedules and availability; therefore, it is recommended that shorter and succinct forms of awareness raising such as meetings, debates, and *workshops be* used.

However, it is the results presented that best convince the High Administration and the managers, as to the relevance of this auditing activity.

As work is done and delivered with quality, clients will see the added value and recognize that we are effectively contributing to the solution of the problem. They will also become ambassadors for the unit and will advocate strongly for doing this kind of work.

Remember that "advertising is the soul of business," so whenever you have the opportunity, encourage, explain, defend, and promote consulting work.

5.4 Technical training of auditors

It is important to reinforce that it is no use having auditors involved and managers aware if the technical staff is not prepared to develop the work.

Thus, it is necessary to provide auditors with the set of technical skills required for effective service development.

There are two main approaches related to technical training: the first refers to understanding and comprehending the consulting process, and the second, to knowing the object to be examined in consulting.

5.4.1 Knowledge about the consulting process

Knowing about the consulting process is paramount to the success of the work. The consulting activity is closely linked to ethical conduct, independence, and objectivity. So, to know consulting is, before anything else, to know, understand, and practice these postures required from the auditor. It is also to deeply know the workflow of auditing and its relationship with the institutional mission.

This type of training can be offered in the way presented in item 5.1 of this chapter or by means of specific courses, made available in the face-to-face or distance learning modality.

5.4.2 Technical knowledge of the consulting object

When starting consulting work, it is possible that not all the team members have adequate technical knowledge related to the object of the work. Therefore, specific training must be provided to enable the effective provision of the service.

For example, when performing risk management consulting work, not all team members may have knowledge of COSO ERM (*Enterprise Risk Management*)[9] or NBR - Brazilian Standard ISO 31.000, which are the main *frameworks* used as risk management models.

In this case, before starting the work, it is essential that the servers participate in specific training activities in order to obtain the necessary technical knowledge.

This training can be offered face-to-face or remotely, *in company* or through courses offered to the external public by government or private schools, or through the transfer of knowledge: when a trained officer of the unit shares his knowledge with other team members.

It is worth noting that according to IPPF standard 1210. C1, the *chief audit executive must decline the consulting engagement or obtain competent advice and assistance if the internal auditors lack the knowledge, skills, or other competencies needed to perform all or part of the engagement.*

Therefore, consulting work can only be accepted when the staff has all the knowledge and skills necessary for its execution.

5.5 TECHNICAL TRAINING AND THE ANNUAL CONSULTING PLAN

When dealing with consulting planning in the next chapter, it will be detailed that consulting work must be planned

---

[9] Available at: https://www.coso.org/documents/coso-erm-executive-summary-portuguese.pdf.

each year and included in the auditor's annual planning, so that the team can prepare for the provision of this service.

In this way, the accomplishment of the work is conditioned to the fulfillment of the requirements, among which is the offering of the necessary training by the organization.

Thus, for a consulting process included in the plan to be effectively executed, it is necessary that the officers are trained according to the needs specified by the audit unit in a training plan, according to what is set forth in the annual planning.

CHAPTER 6

CONSULTING FORECASTING AND PLANNING

As far as consulting is concerned, planning is a management tool that aims to establish, in a systematic way, the steps, procedures, and all the other mechanisms that will be used in the development of the work.

Not only in auditing, but also in other areas of the Brazilian Public Administration, the planning phase is often left in the background, and the execution of the activity becomes the most important part of the process.

This culture of "no planning" causes several consequences, among them the non-achievement of objectives, unnecessary expenses, squandering of public funds, and rework, among others.

To be successful in providing consulting services, it is necessary to set aside adequate time for planning the work, since this is a relatively new process, demanding greater detail in the way the activity is to be executed.

There are three main instruments for planning consulting work: long-term planning, annual planning (forecast of the work in the annual plan), and the planning of each consulting engagement.

In this chapter, we will detail how to plan consulting through these three documents.

6.1 Long-term Planning

The purpose of long-term planning is to establish the IA unit's guidelines and goals for an average period of four years. Since consulting is an internal audit activity, it is included in this plan.

Usually, this planning is reflected in the long-term audit plan, a good practice recommended by the main auditing standards and control bodies.

In the context of consulting work, guidelines are the instructions or indications that set the direction to be followed with regard to this activity. Thus, long-term planning should reflect the unit's guidelines as to the path to be followed in the coming terms.

Examples of guidelines:

Develop the consulting function of internal auditing:

- providing the internal audit unit's staff with the development of knowledge, skills, and attitudes, in order to enable them to implement the internal audit consulting function; and
- ensuring that the auditing, annual reporting, surveys, mandatory analysis, consulting, and monitoring services contribute to the achievement of the established goals and results.

The goals are steps towards the achievement of objectives defined in long-term planning and should be part of the unit's performance indicators. These, in turn, may correspond to a value, a percentage or another unit that measures an aspect of performance, in order to compare this measure with pre-established targets.

Example indicators:

- Indicator: consulting effort in audit activities.

    ☐ Target: allocate 10% of the workforce to perform consulting activities.
- Indicator: quantity of consulting activities carried out by internal auditing.

    ☐ Target: Perform 3 consulting processes per year (Superior Justice Court - Director Plan).[10]

6.2 WORK FORECAST IN THE ANNUAL AUDIT PLANNING

The work forecast occurs through the annual audit plan, which is a formal document produced by the audit unit and approved by the competent authority. The document has the objective of planning the unit's actions for the year, including evaluation, consulting, and other extraordinary activities.

Thus, with regard to the consulting process, all consulting activities approved for the year must be included in the plan, *i.e.* as a rule, consulting actions are approved and included in the annual audit plan for execution during the term of the plan.

It is worth noting that it is possible to perform consulting work that is not previously included in the Annual Audit Plan, but this must be an exceptional case, duly approved by the CAE, with due justification based on technical criteria.

---

[10] Available at: http://www.stj.jus.br/sites/portalp/Transparencia/Auditoria-Interna/Planos-de-auditoria.

In order to include consulting work in the Annual Plan, a request from the competent authority and approval by the head of the internal audit unit is required.

The flow below represents the phases necessary for proper forecasting of consulting work

Chart 14 - Consultancy forecast workflow in the AAP

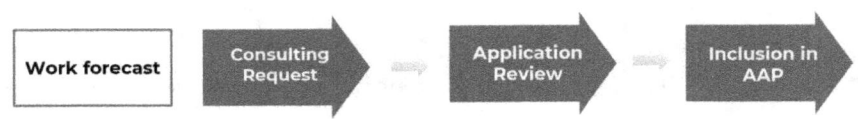

Source: Prepared by the author

6.2.1 Consulting request

The request is the formal request made by the competent authority, containing the necessary elements that allow the evaluation as to the adequacy, pertinence, and relevance of the consulting object.

As already mentioned in chapter 4, the internal regulations must define who are the competent bodies and authorities to submit consulting requests.

Moreover, it is recommended that this prerogative be restricted to the superior officers of the bodies that comprise the organization's High Administration or the board. This does not prevent managers from the tactical and operational rankings from submitting their demands to the High Administration, who, if it agrees, will issue the appropriate request to the audit unit.

For the request to be evaluated, it is necessary to observe the existence of at least the following elements:

- requesting unit;
- date of the request;
- object of the consulting service;
- objective of the consulting service;
- description of the request;
- expected products; and
- expected results.

In the case of facilitation-type consulting services, the application process may be so simplified that not all the requirements of the previous paragraph are required. However, it is important that a request exists, even if it is an invitation by e-mail, memorandum, order, or other mechanism deemed sufficient and appropriate.

For the other types, it is relevant that the application meets all the requirements.

Requesting Unit

The requesting unit is the client of the work, this information is relevant to evaluate if the requesting authority has the legitimacy to request the activity.

Request date

The date of the request is relevant for deadline tracking, to identify the time spent for example in evaluating the request.

Object of consulting

Object of consulting refers to the central topic on which advice will be given. For example, when consulting on the organization's risk management process, the object or central theme will be exactly the organization's risk management process.

Remember that the three macro-objects for consulting work are: governance processes, risk management processes, and controls processes. However, as specified in Chapter 3, it is possible to extract smaller objects, always having as a source the three listed above.

Objective of the requested work

Objective is the reason for the work requested, it is what is intended to be achieved with the execution of the activity.

Description of the Request

This item is where the consulting request is made. E.g.: *I request the offer of consulting work, by the Internal Audit unit, aiming at assisting the Administration in the implementation of the risk management process in the Institution.*

Expected products

Products are the deliverables of the consulting team, what will be produced during the work. Examples of products are a report, a training session, an orientation, an advisory document, an informative, a plan, a program, a guide, a map, or any other previously agreed upon with the client unit.

Please note that, in the first moment, the manager may list the products he considers pertinent; however, when planning the work, and in common agreement between the parties, it is possible, and sometimes even necessary, to agree upon the delivery of products other than those requested here.

Expected Results

At this point, the requesting party must establish the results that are intended to be achieved with the execution of the work, including the expected products and forms of delivery and communication of results.

Additional Information

Additional information is any other data that is relevant and necessary for the proper understanding and limitation of the work.

The following is a sample form with an example of a consulting request.

Chart 15 - Consulting Request Template

EXAMPLE OF AN AUDIT CONSULTING REQUEST	
REQUESTING UNIT:	STRATEGIC MANAGEMENT SECRETARIAT
DATE OF THE REQUEST:	22/02/2022
OBJECT OF CONSULTING Cases cannot be the subject of consultations that: a) decide on a concrete case; b) deal with mere normative interpretation; c) compromise the independence and objectivity of the unit; d) may cause administrative co-management; and e) the management itself can implement independently of the audit.	Risk Management Process
THE OBJECT OF CONSULTING IS RELATED TO THE FOLLOWING MACROPROCESS:	(X) Risk Management ( ) Governance ( ) Internal controls
CONSULTING OBJECTIVE:	Assisting the Administration in implementing risk management in the institution.
DESCRIPTION OF THE REQUEST:	I request that Internal Audit provide consulting services to assist management in the implementation of the risk management process in the institution.

CHAPTER 6 - CONSULTING FORECASTING AND PLANNING

EXPECTED PRODUCTS:	Risk Management Policy; Risk Management Manual; and Knowledge Transfer
EXPECTED RESULTS:	As a result of this consulting, it is expected that the risk management process in the organization will be improved.
ADDITIONAL INFORMATION: any other data relevant and necessary for the proper understanding and limitation of the work	
SIGNATURE PERSON RESPONSIBLE FOR THE REQUEST	

Source: Prepared by the author

6.2.2 Application Review

The evaluation of the application or its admissibility consists of checking whether the application contains all the elements mentioned in 6.2.1, as well as whether it meets the requirements of adequacy, relevance and pertinence for the object of consulting, and should consider at least the following requirements:

Table 16 - Admissibility Requirements

- **01 Requesting competence** — It is related to who has the prerogative to request the consulting work
- **02 Thematic adequacy** — Refers to the possible objects of consulting work
- **03 Technical capability** — It is related to the set of skills, knowledge, and attitudes necessary for the proper provision of the service
- **04 Operational capability** — Refers to the availability of employees compared to the number of activities planned for the activity
- **05 Potential of the work** — Refers to the potential contributions of the work for the improvement of internal processes

APPLICATION REVIEW

Source: Prepared by the author

Requesting competence

Competence relates to who has the prerogative to request consulting work. Thus, if the organization's auditing standards have established that only the High Administration is competent to request this type of work and the request has been made by a different authority, the request will not be approved due to defective competence.

It is worth mentioning that, if consulting is proposed by the internal audit unit itself, there must be interaction with the High Administration, in order to obtain their agreement for the immediate provision of the service or inclusion in the Annual Audit Plan.

Thematic adequacy

Thematic adequacy refers to the objects subject to consulting work. As previously studied, processes related to governance, risk management, and internal controls can be submitted to the consulting. Thus, if the request does not refer to one of these topics, it cannot be approved.

Technical capability

The unit's technical capability is related to the set of skills, knowledge, and attitudes necessary for the proper provision of the service.

In this regard, IPPF 1210.C1 established that the chief audit executive must decline consulting engagements, or obtain competent advice and assistance, if internal auditors do not have the knowledge, skills or other competencies necessary to perform all or part of the engagement.

Operational capability

On the other hand, operational capability refers to the availability of employees compared to the number of activities planned for the unit, that is, whether there enough professionals to develop the tasks already planned and the consulting process without compromising the audit results.

Potential of the work

The potential refers to the ability of the results of the work to contribute to the improvement of the institution's risk management, controls and governance processes. The IPPF 2010.C1 (2017) standard prescribes that the chief audit executive should base himself, when considering the acceptance of proposals for consulting engagements, on the potential of these engagements to improve risk management, to add value and improve the organization's operations.

After evaluating all these criteria, the chief audit executive will approve or not the inclusion of the works in the annual audit plan.

If the number of requests that meet all the admissibility criteria exceeds the unit's capability, a method may be adopted to select the objects to be included in the annual plan. This method must take into account:

- the potential of the work to improve governance processes, risk management, and controls (added value);
- the technical and operational capability of the team;
- the risk involved in not improving the process;
- the degree of transversal impact of the process; and
- alignment with the organization's strategic planning.

Regarding the first two questions, these have already been duly described in the previous items of this chapter.

Regarding the risks arising from the non-improvement of the process, the possible negative impacts must be evaluated, if the referred counseling is not provided.

With regard to the degree of transversal impact of the process, it must be evaluated whether the process covers only a specific area of the organization, some sectors or all units of the institution.

Regarding the alignment with the strategic planning, it must be verified if the object is related to the organizational strategy.

Acceptance of the work must be communicated to the client and the work included in the Annual Audit Plan.

Below is a model form containing a practical example of analysis of the consulting request:

Table 17 - Request model and analysis

REQUEST ANALYSIS EXAMPLE	
REQUESTING UNIT (item 2.7):	STRATEGIC MANAGEMENT SECRETARIAT
CONSULTANCY OBJECT:	Risk Management Process
CONSULTANCY OBJECTIVE:	Assisting the Administration in the implementation of risk management in the institution.
REQUEST DESCRIPTION:	This is a request from the Strategic Management Secretariat for this audit unit to provide consulting services with the objective of assisting Management in the implementation of the risk management process in the Institution.
PRODUCTS PROVIDED BY THE AUDIT:	Assistance in the development of a Risk Management Policy; Assistance in the development of a Risk Management manual; Knowledge transfer about Risk Management to those involved in the process; and A report containing the result of the work.
EXPECTED RESULTS	It is expected that consulting may help Management in the effective implementation of the risk management process in the body, so that a risk management system is established that allows and helps managers to identify, evaluate, treat and monitor significant risks, thus contributing to the achievement of institutional objectives.

REQUEST ASSESSMENT	
REQUESTING COMPETENCE (ITEM 2.8):	Does the requesting authority have the authority to request consulting engagements? (X) Yes ( ) No
THEMATIC ADEQUACY (ITEM	Is the subject of the work subject to consultation? (X) Yes ( ) No If not, indicate the circumstance of framing the object: ( ) This is a concrete case; ( ) It compromises the independence and objectivity of the audit unit; ( ) This is administrative co-management; ( ) This is a mere normative interpretation; ( ) Management can implement independent internal audit improvement; ( ) The object is not associated with governance, risks or internal controls; ( ) Another, justify:
TECHNICAL CAPABILITY:	Does the consulting team have the technical capability to provide the service? (X) Yes ( ) No
OPERATIONAL CAPABILITY:	Does the audit unit have the capacity to assign the necessary workforce to provide the consulting service? (X) Yes ( ) No
POTENTIAL OF THE WORK	Does the result of the work have the potential to add value and improve the organization's processes? (X) Yes ( ) No

INTERNAL AUDIT OPINION REGARDING THE ADMISSIBILITY OF THE SERVICE:	The work must: ( ) Be admitted and included in the Annual Audit Plan; or ( ) Be admitted and performed in the present year or ( ) NOT be admitted.

JUSTIFICATION FOR ADMISSION OR NOT TO WORK	Considering that the request meets all the requirements established for the provision of a service of an advisory nature and that:
	  i) it is not an ongoing process (specific case);
	  ii) it does not refer to legal analysis or normative interpretation;
	  iii) the subjects dealt with are directly related to the strategic planning of the agency, with great potential to add value and improve organizational processes, improving their controls; and
	  iv) the nature of the work will not result in the auditor's loss of objectivity, as it is not a management act.; and
	  v) the object is related to risk management, object of mandatory analysis of the audit.
	The present work is admitted, which should be included in the Annual Audit Planning so that it can be planned and executed in the next term.

SIGNATURE RESPONSIBLE FOR THE EVALUATION	

Source: Prepared by the author

So far, the focus has been on multi-year planning and annual audit planning.

From this point on, the planning of the consulting action will be approached, of the individual work itself, which, among all, is the most detailed of the plans.

The planning of the consulting work aims to establish its objective, outline its scope, define the methodological strategy to be adopted and estimate the resources, costs and timeline necessary for its accomplishment; in addition to establishing the main risks involved and the expected results.

The planning of the consulting action is concluded with a document called "consulting program".

6.2.3 CONSULTING PROGRAM

The consulting program is a formal document, prepared by the internal audit unit and accepted by the client, which may have the following elements:

- object of consulting;
- preliminary object information;
- objective;
- roles and responsibilities;
- scope;
- no-scope;
- type of consulting;
- expected benefits;
- necessary resources;

- applicable criteria;
- methodology/operation strategy;
- expected products;
- ways of communicating the results;
- consulting risk matrix; and
- timeline.

Consulting object

The consulting object has already been described in item 6.2.1.1, however, if the request has not properly established the object, it must be adequate when preparing the consulting program.

Preliminary object information

Preliminary information on the object consists of collecting the most relevant data related to the object of the consulting, in order to better establish the scope, methodology and procedures necessary for an efficient consulting.

Preliminary information must contain data such as: the definition of the object, main legal and regulatory requirements, applicable regulations and frameworks, a summary of the control bodies' vision and literature findings.

Objective

As already established in item 6.2.1.2, the objective is the raison d'être of the activity, it is what is intended to be achieved with the execution of this type of work, it is its target, its purpose, its purpose.

Roles and responsibilities

This is one of the main items of a consulting program, since it is in this opportunity that the roles and responsibilities of the parties involved are recorded.

In this item, it must be stated that the auditor does not assume any responsibility that belongs to the manager.

It should also provide that the consulting work is opinionated advice, and the manager must decide whether or not to adopt the advice or result presented.

It can also be mentioned that the consulting is not an impediment for the consulted process to be the object of an evaluation action by the audit unit.

This item can also predict whether possible recommendations from the unit will be subject to future monitoring.

In addition to those exemplified above, the document should contain all roles and responsibilities relevant to the specific consulting process.

Scope

In the consulting program developed by the audit unit, the scope should be as detailed as possible, in order to clearly define the scope and limits of the work.

Defining the scope is a relevant task within the planning process, as it mitigates a series of risk events inherent to the activity.

When defining the scope, the extent of the work, what is covered in the activity and everything else that is necessary to establish the appropriate limit of action must be made clear, so as not to compromise the independence and objectivity of the unit.

Non-scope

Another relevant part of the Consulting Program refers to the non-scope, that is, what will not be the object of advice.

The non-scope is what, given the object of consulting, could lead to the understanding that it is covered in the work, but, due to technical or operational incapacity, or because it is not timely, it will not be addressed in the counseling. In fact, non-scoping is an effort to align expectations of both sides with the actual work to be developed.

Type of consulting service

Consulting types have already been covered in detail in Chapter 2, which is why we will not cover them at this point.

Expected benefits

Expected benefits are what is expected from the implementation of counseling, what is intended to be achieved by offering the job. The benefits are directly related to the aggregation of value and, consequently, with the achievement of the objective of the consulting. So, for example, a consulting to improve an organization's hiring process could bring the benefit of faster hiring, leading to financial savings, or better use of the workforce, avoiding rework and delay in completing the process. Or it can provide more efficient hiring free of material distortions caused by error or fraud.

Necessary resources

Specification of human, financial, technological or any other resources necessary for the proper provision of the consulting service.

Applicable criteria

Criteria in consulting is the required or desired state of the object of the work, that is, it is the norm, the standard, the policy, the good practice or any mechanism used as a parameter to propose a solution to improve the object consulted.

Thus, a consulting on the Risk Management Process, for example, could have as criteria: the NBR ISO 31000 Standard, or the COSO ERM model, or a risk management policy of a specific body identified as a good practice through benchmarking.

Criteria in an evaluation process do not differ in essence from those used in a consulting process. The difference is in the approach. While in an evaluation process the criteria are used, as a rule, to identify an inconsistency, divergence, inadequacy, etc., in a consulting, the criterion is used as a parameter for proposing solutions, that is, the same COSO ERM can be used to identify an opportunity for improvement in an evaluation process and to be the opportunity for improvement in a consulting process.

Methodology/operation strategy

Methodology is the establishment of the form of execution of the work from the planning to the delivery of the results and comprises all the methods to be used in the collection and evaluation of information, in the performance of benchmarking and interviews, in the use of tools and frameworks or any other another method that may be used during consulting.

In addition to the methodology, the unit's operating strategy can be established, whether the result will be presented only at the end or partially, whether various types of consulting will be adopted or a single specific type and, also, what form of interaction and contribution of the unit will be client, or any other strategy that the auditing unit intends to use during the provision of the service.

Timeline

The timeline is the tool in which the workforce reserved for the performance of the work, the stages, the respective deadlines and those responsible for each activity are established.

Consulting risk matrix

Each consulting engagement must contain the survey, assessment and treatment of process-specific risks.

Thus, the planning of each engagement must contain the appropriate risk matrix with the respective events and the assessment of the impact and probability of their occurrence, as well as the controls to be implemented to mitigate those identified as being of greater relevance.

It is worth mentioning that the matrix specified in the paragraph above refers to the risks of consulting work in that specific object.

Thus, when developing consulting services to improve the organization's risk management process, for example, a risk matrix should be prepared containing the risk events to which that work is subject.

It is not, therefore, the risk of the consulting object, but the risk of offering work for that specific object.

Planned products

This item specifies the products and by-products to be delivered at the end of the work, as previously discussed, the product can be a report, training, guidance, an advisory document, a newsletter, a plan, a program, a guide, a map, or any other previously adjusted with the client unit of the job.

This item is strongly linked to the alignment of expectations between parties, which may shape the scope and non-scope, in order to make clear what is intended with the performance of the work.

Ways to communicate results

The form of communication of the results is directly related to the type and to the expected results generated by the consulting.

At this point, I will not delve into the aforementioned topic, considering that Chapter 8 deals specifically with the way of communicating the results of the consulting work.

The following is a model consulting program containing all the topics specified in the item above

Table 18 - Consulting Program Model

SUMMARY

PRESENTATION

[Presentation of what the report is about, the type of work, who requested and who approved the offer of consultation, preferably referencing the respective acts]

PRELIMINARY OBJECT INFORMATION

[The preliminary information must contain data such as definition of the object, main requirements required by laws, regulations and specific frameworks, a summary of the control bodies' vision and literature findings. Finally, a view of the object must be presented in the organ of the consulted object]

OBJECTIVE

[Specify the objective of the activity, which is nothing more than the reason for being of the requested work, it is what is intended to be achieved with the execution of the activity.]

SCOPE AND NON SCOPE OF THE CONSULTANCY

[The scope must detail the scope of the work, what is covered in the activity and everything else that is necessary to establish the appropriate limit of action, so as not to compromise, mainly, the independence and objectivity of the unit.

The non-scope is what, given the object of consulting, could lead to the understanding that it is covered in the work, but, due to technical or operational incapacity, or because it is not timely, it will not be addressed in the counseling. In fact, non-scoping is an effort to delimit the expectations of both sides with the work to be done.]

ROLES AND RESPONSIBILITIES

[In this item, it should be stated that the auditor does not assume any responsibility that belongs to the Administration and its managers. It should also provide that the consulting work is guiding advice, and the manager must decide whether or not to adopt the advice or result presented. It can also be mentioned that the consulting is not an impediment for the consulted process to be the object of an evaluation action by the audit unit. This item can also predict whether possible recommendations from the unit will be subject to future monitoring. In addition to those exemplified above, the document should contain all roles and responsibilities relevant to the specific consulting process.]

OPERATION METHODOLOGY AND STRATEGY

[In this topic, the way in which the work is carried out from planning to delivery of results must be established and comprises all the methods to be used in the collection and evaluation of information, in the performance of benchmarking and interviews, in the use of tools and frameworks or of any other method that may be used during the consulting work. In addition to the methodology, the unit's operating strategy can be established, whether the result will be presented only at the end or partially, whether various types of consulting will be adopted or a single specific type and, also, what form of interaction and contribution of the unit will be client, or any other strategy that the auditing unit intends to use during the provision of the service.]

CRITERIA

[Here, the norm, standard, policy, good practice or any mechanism that will be used as a parameter to propose solutions that improve the consulted object must be established.]

EXPECTED RESULTS

[This item must demonstrate the expected results and the products that will be delivered at the end of the activity.]

RISK AND CONTROLS MATRIX

[In this item, the matrix of risks and controls specific to the consulting work must be inserted]

TIMELINE

PLANNING - specify required workforce		
Activities	servers	Estimated duration
EXECUTION - specify required workforce		
COMMUNICATION OF RESULTS - specify required workforce		
CONSULTING TEAM		

Other information relevant to the planning phase, but which does not need to be included in the program, is information on labor costs. Thus, whenever possible, the costs of developing the consulting activity should be measured.

In cases where the organization does not have an adequate cost system, a simplified methodology may be used.

It is worth noting that this is managerial information for audit decision-making, and the unit must define the best way to use and disclose it.

After the consulting program has been prepared, a Term of Commitment must be signed with the client unit, since the consulting process is an agreement between the parties and, if the requesting area does not comply with the terms established by the audit, the program must be agreed upon or the work cannot be performed.

Below is a model form containing an example of a Term of Commitment after preparing the Consulting Program

Table 19 - Model of Term of Commitment AFTER elaboration of the Consulting Program

EXAMPLE OF TERM OF COMMITMENT (WITH CONSULTING PROGRAM)	
APPLICANT UNIT:	STRATEGIC MANAGEMENT SECRETARIAT
WORK OBJECTIVE:	To assist the Administration in the implementation of risk management in the institution.

DECLARATION OF ACCEPTANCE OF THE CONSULTANCY PROGRAM TERMS:	The Consulting Program presented established the object, defining the scope, the objectives of the work, the expected results and the products to be delivered, according to the type of consulting defined, the schedule of activities, and, mainly, the roles and responsibilities of all those involved in the process, making it clear what is the responsibility of the audit and what is the exclusive responsibility of the manager with regard to the planned work. Thus, this Administration unit agrees with the terms proposed and specified in said Consulting Program.
SIGNATURE RESPONSIBLE FOR THE REQUEST	

Source: Prepared by the author

It is worth noting that, in the event of signing the Term of Commitment prior to the preparation of the consulting program or equivalent document, that Term must contain all the necessary requirements for understanding the object and the roles and responsibilities of the parties involved.

Therefore, the term of commitment in this case must contain at least the following elements:

- Type of consulting;
- Expected products
- Expected results
- Scope and general methodology

CHAPTER 6 - CONSULTING FORECASTING AND PLANNING

- not scope
- Roles and responsibilities
- Form of communication of results
- Information whether or not there will be recommendations
- Information whether or not there will be monitoring

It is important to note here that, in the case of signing the term of commitment before the Consulting Program, effective preliminary analysis of the object and the involvement of the client of the work is essential, because, without knowing the object and without involving the client, it is not possible to establish the requirements mentioned in the paragraph above.

Below is an example of a Term of Commitment signed before the preparation of the Consulting Program or equivalent document

Table 20 - Term of Commitment Template WITHOUT drafting of the Consulting Program

EXAMPLE OF TERM OF COMMITMENT (WITHOUT CONSULTING PROGRAM)	
INTRODUCTION: Explain the object of the consulting, its general objective, its importance and the reason. Inform here if the execution of the consulting will be simple or combined (consulting and evaluation)	This is a request from the Strategic Management Secretariat for this auditing unit to offer consulting work aimed at assisting the Administration in the implementation of the risk management process in the Institution.
CONSULTANCY TYPE:	(x) Counsel ( ) Advice ( ) Facilitation ( ) Training
EXPECTED PRODUCTS:	Assisting in the development of a Risk Management Policy; Assisting in the development of a Risk Management manual; Transferring knowledge about Risk Management to those involved in the process; and Issuing a report containing the result of the work.
EXPECTED RESULTS:	It is expected that the consulting may help Management in the effective implementation of the risk management process in the body, so that a risk management system is established that allows and helps managers to identify, assess, treat and monitor significant risks, thus contributing to the achievement of institutional objectives.

SCOPE AND GENERAL METHODOLOGY:	The scope of this consulting is to assist the administration in the implementation of risk management in the organization. The assistance will be offered through the support offered for the development of the Risk Management Policy and a Risk Management manual. In addition, the audit team will promote the transfer of knowledge about Risk Management to those involved in the process. At the end of the work, a report will be issued consolidating all the information and those related to the object and the results obtained with the accomplishment of the work. The present work began with the preliminary analysis for knowledge of the object, which consisted of collecting information on risk management and surveying the current maturity of risk management in the unit. Then, a wide collection and analysis of data will be carried out with benchmarking, survey and analysis of the main frameworks related to the subject, bibliographic and doctrinal research, jurisprudence of the Court of Auditors, normative references and established criteria including good practices, as well as the survey and analysis of policies and manuals used by the main Brazilian public organizations. After performing the work and communicating the results, a transfer of knowledge will be offered to those responsible for coordinating and implementing risk management on the subject. In meetings, workshops, debates and documents, advice will be offered that will help the client in the elaboration of the draft policy and risk management manual. After the counseling, a consulting report will be issued and forwarded to High Administration and all those involved in the risk management process, for knowledge and appreciation.

NO SCOPE:	The responsibility for the implementation and coordination of risk management is not part of the scope of this consulting Also, the implementation of controls to ensure the effectiveness of risk management, definition of risk appetite and treatment for each assessed risk, among other typical management activities, does not constitute the scope of the work.

CHAPTER 6 - CONSULTING FORECASTING AND PLANNING

ROLES AND RESPONSIBILITIES:	Internal Audit Responsibilities: a) to perform the advisory services in accordance with the agreements established with the client unit and with due proficiency and professional zeal; b) to deliver the results in the manner and within the term stipulated in this Term of Commitment or in another adjusted document, keeping the Unit informed about the occurrence of any situation that may impact the established planning; c) to provide advice, through assistance in the development of the Risk Management Policy and the Risk Management manual; and d) to promote the transfer of knowledge in relation to the Risk Management process of the organization in the form agreed with the client in this term of commitment or in another adjustment made. Internal Audit reserves the right to: a) establish the auditing techniques that it deems necessary for the proper performance of the consulting services; b) communicate to the Unit's High Administration when the nature and materiality or the results of the work represent significant risks to the organization; c) interrupt or suspend the work in the event of identification of illegal or irregular acts or facts that impact the execution of consulting services, as well as their eventual investigation; and d) in the future, promote an evaluation action in the risk management process, not being a valid argument, in the evaluation or other activity, the information that a certain act or fact has been or has not been performed due to the consulting process offered by the Audit Internal. This is because the responsibility for implementing controls always rests with the organization's management. Administration Responsibilities: e) to timely ensure the availability of information, assets and personnel necessary for the execution of the works; f) to coordinate the risk management process. As the audit is only responsible for assisting the coordinating unit in the implementation of the necessary mechanisms for an effective risk management; g) to prepare the drafts of the Risk Management Policy and the Risk Management Manual, whether or not to use the advice offered by the audit during the execution of the advisory work; h) to decide whether or not to implement the advice resulting from the consulting process offered; i) to decide on the actions taken as a result of the advice resulting from the consulting service; j) to implement any and all controls aimed at ensuring the effectiveness of the risk management process.

HOW WILL THE RESULTS BE COMMUNICATED?	(X) Report (X) Minutes of Meeting (X) Consulting Notes (X) Training ( ) Guides. References Booklets. Guidance ( ) Others. Please specify:
TO WHOM WILL THE RESULTS BE FORWARDED?	( ) Advice (X) High Administration (X) Process Managers ( ) Every Organization ( ) Internal Public ( ) Published on the Internet ( ) Others. Please specify:
WILL THE FINAL REPORT CONTAIN RECOMMENDATIONS?	( ) Yes (X) No
WILL THERE BE WORK MONITORING?	( ) Yes (X) No
DEADLINES AND SCHEDULE: Register the activities that will be developed the deadlines	Planning: Start: 03/02/2022; End: 04/02/2022 Execution: Start: 04/03/2022 End: 06/02/2022 Communication of Results: Start: 06/03/2022; End 02/07/2022
FINAL REMARKS Inform any other specific points that are relevant to the execution of the works.	
DECLARATION OF ACCEPTANCE OF THE TERM OF COMMITMENT.	The Internal Audit Secretariat and the Strategic Management Secretariat express themselves in accordance with this Term of Commitment

Accordingly.

Place and date

Signature Responsible Title of the Manager in charge	Signature Responsible Title of the Auditor in charge

CHAPTER 7

EXECUTION OF THE CONSULTING WORK

As seen in the previous chapter, the planning of the consulting work ends with the drafting of the consulting program. Consulting itself starts after the signing of the Term of Commitment.

The implementation process consists of applying the methodology and procedures established in the program, and must conform to the different types of consulting: counsel, advice, facilitation, training, and combined.

It is worth noting that during this phase it is possible to adapt the program to include or remove procedures to make the consulting process more efficient.

Basically, there are two ways of executing consulting work: single execution and joint execution.

In simple execution, the advice is planned and executed in a stand-alone manner, without involving evaluation work. In other words, it is pure consulting without any prior or concomitant evaluation work.

Joint execution refers to combining an evaluation with one or more of the types of consulting services specified above, *i.e.* initially an evaluation of the governance, risk management, or control processes is carried out, and then the advice is given, through consulting services, to improve the evaluated object.

The advantage of joint consulting is that the previous evaluation will help the team to understand the process and the opportunities for improvement, before starting consulting.

An example of this type of consulting would be an audit aimed at evaluating the maturity of the organization's risk management and, after the evaluation, to offer a type of consulting (advice, facilitation, or training) to improve the evaluated process.

Thus, this chapter will focus on issues about the execution of the procedures planned for the consulting work.

7.1 EXECUTION OF COUNSEL-TYPE CONSULTING SERVICES

To visualize the workflow of counsel-type consulting, see the chart below:

Table 21 - Counsel-type consulting execution workflow

![Counsel-type consulting execution workflow diagram showing three rows: DATA COLLECTION (Selection of Standards, Processes, Frameworks, Maps, Best Practices → Questionnaire Application and Benchmarking → Brainstorming, Stakeholder Interviews → Additional Data Collection Techniques); DATA ANALYSIS (Applying Data Analysis Techniques → Discussion of possible solutions); SOLUTION PROPOSITION (Selection of feasible solutions → Discussion of proposals with the Client → Proposing Solutions)]

Source: Prepared by the author

As shown above, the execution of this type of consulting has 3 distinct phases: data collection, data analysis, and solution proposition.

Data collection in consulting is no different from that used in evaluation work; it is about obtaining the necessary information to understand the object and to propose effective solutions. To this end, specific auditing techniques are used, which will be explained later in this chapter.

As far as data analysis is concerned, this is the application of techniques, aiming at extracting the necessary information from the collected data. This information will subsidize the proposition of effective solutions that guarantee the fulfillment of the consulting work's objective; these techniques will be described and defined in due course.

First, however, I will repeat here an example of consulting already described in Chapter 2, but which helps to better understand how this type of consulting is carried out.

This is an example of consulting advice to improve the organization's risk management process.

In this activity, the audit could initially gather all relevant information about the risk management process in the organizations, such as: norms, standards, models, *frameworks,* flows, processes, maps, best practices, and everything necessary for the investigation and proposition of effective solutions by the work team.

After receiving this information it is up to the auditors to analyze and understand it so that they are ready to discuss and propose solutions.

Regarding the products to be generated by the consulting, the team could, based on the studies and understanding of the object, assist the organization in developing or updating the mapping of the main organizational processes or macroprocesses.

Second, it could transfer knowledge to the team members involved in the risk management process.

Third, the audit would help in identifying good practices such as policies, plans, manuals, and tools that could be adopted by the agency.

Finally, the audit would assist the organization in developing the risk management policy and risk management manual, helping and guiding the production of documents in each of their phases.

Note that responsibility for preparing the drafts lies with the Administration. The IA unit merely counsels, advises and guides the Administration to build the product.

It should be noted that the Administration being responsible for the preparation of the drafts does not prevent the IA unit from suggesting topics, models, texts, and everything else it deems pertinent to the composition of the drafts.

It is up to the Administration to decide whether the proposed advice will be part of the drafts to be developed. At the end of the work, a consulting report could be generated to record all the advice proposed by the work team.

Note that, in this example, at least five products could be generated: assistance with process mapping, knowledge transfer, presentation of policy and manual templates, assistance with drafting the risk management policy, assistance with drafting the risk management procedures manual, and the final consulting report.

It is also possible to visualize multiple other products, such as encouragement to create a risk management structure, facilitation of the risk management committee, help in developing tools for identifying, analyzing, treating, and reporting on risks, and the production of a guideline document that will continue to improve the solution developed.

Of course, the case above is merely an example, and it is possible and plausible to visualize countless ways and strategies to conduct counsel-type consulting. In each case, and in agreement with the client, the products to be generated by the consulting team must be defined based on the intended results.

The previous example can be replicated for several consulting objects, always related to governance, risk management, and internal controls, given the objective of each consulting and the specificity of each object.

Regarding the various types of documents that can be used in the communication of consulting results, in the next chapter we will deal in detail with this subject.

7.1.1 Consulting Techniques

As already seen in the previous chapter, counsel-type consulting is the most complex audit consulting activity. Because of that, a wide range of consulting techniques may be employed.

The main techniques that can be used in this type of consulting work are related to those used in evaluation services, after the necessary adjustments and adaptations

It is not the purpose of this book to exhaustively describe how to use each of the techniques listed here, but rather to exemplify the various techniques that can be used in a consulting process.

The table below exemplifies the consulting techniques:

Chart 22 - Examples of Consulting Techniques,

Examples of Consulting Techniques

1. **Benchmarking** — Mechanism for identifying and implementing good practices
2. **Frameworks Analysis** — Evaluating various models and standards related to the object of work
3. **Document Analysis** — Examination of documents contained in processes, computerized systems, or any other system that makes use of information relevant to the work
4. **Reference Panel** — Obtaining the opinion of experienced professionals in relation to the subject matter of the consultation
5. **Focus Group** — A tool for collecting data from the interactions and discussions that take place in a group
6. **Environment Analysis** — Stakeholder analysis, SWOT analysis. Process Mapping
7. **RACI Analysis** — Identifying the responsibility for decisions and execution of activities as well as the type or degree of participation
8. **Direct Observation** — It is related to the auditor's power of visual observation
9. **Interviews** — Q&A sessions to obtain specific information
10. **Problem Analysis** — Problem Analysis. Ishikawa diagram, Problem tree, Bow tie method

Source: Prepared by the author

Environment Analysis

Environment analysis consists of enabling internal auditors to better understand the environment inherent to the object of the consulting work, in order to enable the appropriate direction of the service offered.

For the proper outlining and sizing of the counseling object, scenario analyses and other techniques make it possible to exhaustively investigate the work environment surrounding the object.

To this end, the following techniques, among others, may be adopted: (a) *stakeholder* analysis, (b) *SWOT* analysis, and (c) process mapping.

It is worth emphasizing that environmental analysis must be performed during the planning phase of the work, in order to correctly estimate the size of the service in the consulting program.

Also, if the analysis has not been sufficiently deep during the planning phase, it must be complemented at the beginning of the execution of the work.

a) Stakeholder analysis

The *stakeholder* analysis consists of identifying the main actors involved in the consulting process, as well as verifying the interests of each one and how these interests impact the consulting object.

When it comes to the consulting process, stakeholders are all those who have a decisive influence over the success of the work.

b) SWOT Analysis

The best known scenario analysis technique refers to SWOT analysis, which stands for strengths, weaknesses, opportunities, and threats, respectively.

This technique consists in identifying the internal strengths and weaknesses of the organization and the opportunities and threats related to the external environment in which the institution operates.

Although this is a technique widely adopted in strategic planning, in counseling work, the SWOT matrix can also help reveal situations internal strengths or weaknesses, as well as external opportunities and threats of the consulting object.

In summary, it helps identify and implement the most adequate strategy for the consulting service.

c) Process Mapping

Process mapping is a technique to graphically represent operations under consultation. It must include information on: activities, deadlines, participants, and information flow, among other things.

This technique simplifies the process of identifying opportunities for improvement, especially with regard to streamlining and improving the organization's governance, risk management, and control processes.

There are several situations that the maps can represent: from the current processing path (*as is*), to the way recommended by the norms and standards (*to be*), or even the most efficient path, as found by the consulting team.

In short, process mapping is a simple and efficient visualization technique of the entire flow of the object being consulted. It enables better analysis and proposition of the appropriate advice on the subject.

Through the use of the environment analysis techniques specified in this item, it will be possible to know, in a methodological and detailed way, all the main aspects related to the consulting object. This clarifies the best to reach efficiency in the counsel-type consulting process.

Problem Analysis

To be able to offer effective counseling, the consulting team may have to investigate the causes and effects of the problems presented by the object of the work.

In this sense, problem analysis techniques are mechanisms that make it possible to study these problems by comprehensively studying their causes and consequences, as well as the relationship between them.

There are three main problem analysis techniques that can be used in consulting work: Ishikawa diagram, problem tree, and the *Bow tie*.

i. Ishikawa Diagram

The Ishikawa diagram is known as the "cause and effect diagram" or "fishbone diagram" and consists of a method that represents, in graphic form, the possible causes responsible for generating a specific result.

The Ishikawa diagram is a tool that makes it possible to organize the ideas in relation to a certain problem, differentiating what is a cause from what is an effect.

In the diagram, causes or factors are represented by arrows that contribute to the effect (problem) being analyzed. Complex causes or factors can be broken down into details (primary causes and secondary causes), without losing the overall picture.[11]

ii. Problem tree

The problem tree is a participatory technique that assists in developing creative ideas to identify the problem and orga-

---

[11] TCU, 2013 apud DAYCHOUM, 2007, p. 139.

nize the information collected, generating a model of causal relationships that explain the problem. This technique facilitates the identification and organization of the causes and consequences or effects of a central problem.[12]

iii. *Bow tie*

The technique called *Bow tie* is a simple and objective mechanism to exhaustively describe and analyze a risk event, including its causes, prevention and mitigation measures, and possible consequences.

In a consulting process, the use of problem analysis techniques can help the work team to identify the causes and consequences of a presented problem, so they can give advice that effectively leads to the improvement of the consulted process.

Benchmarking

In relation to audit consulting, the *benchmarking* technique can be understood as a mechanism for identifying and implementing good management practices within the public administration.

Its purpose is to allow, to know and to evaluate if good practices developed by other institutions can be adapted and used by client organizations.

Thus, *benchmarking* should answer at least the following questions: What are other bodies and institutiones doing with respect to consulting? Which bodies have already implemented audit consulting? Which entities use best practices applied to this subject? Which of these best practices can be adapted and implemented by the consulting team or unit? How does the

---

[12] TCU, 2013 *apud* COHEN; MARTINEZ, 2004, p. 114.

performance of the consulting unit compare with similar units? Which practices have proved unsuitable and should be avoided?

Augusto Cury, a renowned behavioral author, has a quote that says, "An intelligent person learns from his mistakes, a wise person learns from the mistakes of others. "

Benchmarking allows us to do this: to learn not only from our own mistakes but by evaluating what went right and wrong in other organizations.

The learning generated must be used in all its perspectives, in order to implement what went right and avoid what was unsuccessful.

Benchmarking, if used in the appropriate way, has the potential not only to pave the way for the appropriate improvement of the Administration, but also to generate a much more efficient improvement process. Because the public organizations are funded by public money - which ultimately belongs to the citizen -, when learning is used in another institution, this represents savings for the State as there will be no effort to start a process, but only an adaptation and learning of a process already developed.

For these reasons, *benchmarking* is one of the most efficient consulting techniques in auditing, with the potential to generate new ideas and parameters for the improvement of institutional performance.

Framework Analysis

In addition to *benchmarking*, in many counsel-type consulting processes it is necessary to perform a *framework* analysis, that is, to evaluate the various models and standards related to the organization's governance, risk management, and control processes.

For example, if the consulting process covers the organization's risk management, it will be necessary to evaluate, at a minimum, the COSO ERM and ISO NBR 31000 frameworks, which are the main risk management frameworks currently used by Brazilian public organizations.

In addition, many organizations have chosen to merge two or more management models, thus generating a customized risk management model.

The need to evaluate the various *frameworks* also applies to the governance and controls processes whenever applicable, *i.e.* framework analysis consists in checking and evaluating all the models and performance standards existing in the market and with the potential to contribute to the consulting process.

It is worth pointing out that, when offering consulting work whose framework has already been defined by the client unit, this model must be considered in the work along with contributions from other frameworks.

Document analysis

Document analysis refers to the examination of documents contained in processes, computerized systems, or any other that makes use of information relevant to the consulting work, as occurs during evaluation work.

Reference Panel

In a consulting process, it may be necessary to obtain the opinion of experienced professionals regarding the subject matter of the consultation.

In this sense, the technique called "reference panel" can be used, which is a meeting of experts in a certain area to debate and give their opinion on the matter at hand.

Audit Focus Group

Focus groups can be defined as a tool for collecting data from the interactions and discussions that take place in a group (KRUEGER; CASEY, 2000).

Unlike the reference panel, the technique called "focus group" does not aim to hear experts on the subject, but to involve groups of people with common characteristics. This helps the auditor understand how people perceive a given situation.

This technique, tries to capture the variety of perceptions and ideas of a group about a certain theme or situation, as well as their reasons (MORGAN, 1996).

In a consulting process, Audit Focus Groups are important for collecting qualitative information, especially in situations where there is a need to evaluate aspects related to the attitudes, motivations, and concerns of a specific group.

The technique can be used, for example, to ascertain the values, principles, and opinions of managers, stakeholders, or beneficiaries about the processes or activities related to the object of consulting.

RACI Analysis

RACI stands for Responsible, Accountable, Consulted, and Informed. With this technique, it is possible to establish who is responsible for an activity, who executes it, who is consulted, and who is informed about a process or object analyzed.

In the course of the consulting process, the RACI analysis may help ascertain the responsibility for decisions and the execution of activities, to identify the type or degree of participation of each employee in the decision, to better understand the relationship between the parties involved, and to reveal the distribution of power.

Direct observation in auditing

Direct observation is related to the auditor's power of visual observation.

In the consulting field, it can be useful to identify and better understand the way a process or procedure impacts the consulting object.

Interviews

In short, an interview is a questions and answers session to obtain specific information (ISSAI/Appendix 1, 2004).

In audit consulting, this is one of the most frequently used techniques. During the counsel-type consulting, auditors must obtain information and perceptions from all stakeholders. The interview is one of the most appropriate tools for this type of task.

It is worth pointing out that, contrary to what it may seem, planning and conducting an interview is not a trivial task, requiring the auditor to have the necessary preparation and skills to conduct the process efficiently.

7.2 EXECUTION OF ADVICE-TYPE CONSULTING

As previously discussed in a specific chapter of this book, advice-type consulting begins with a request from the organization or with the decision of the audit unit to provide the work. Usually, the decision to provide advisory services stems from evaluation work or from the knowledge or expertise of the auditor.

The table below presents the relevant workflow of the advice-type consulting.

Table 23 - Flow of execution of the orientation consulting

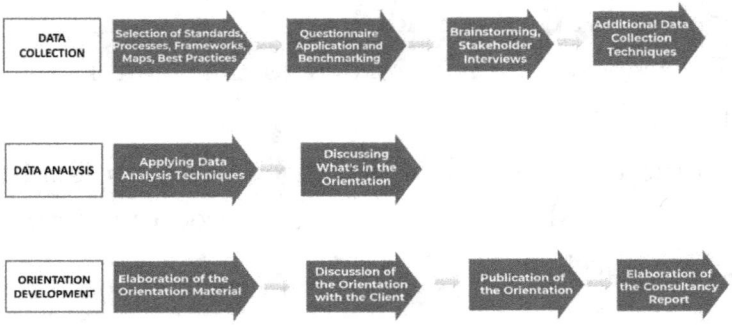

Source: Prepared by the author

As shown in the table above, the phases of data collection and analysis in the execution of the consulting of the advice--type is very similar to that of the counsel-type, differing only with regard to the discussion of proposals. While in the *orientation development phase* (during advice-type consulting) we discuss what will be contained in the orientative document, in the *solution proposition phase* (during counsel-type consulting) we discuss possible solutions to be proposed.

The result of advice-type consulting is the elaboration and publication of some orientative document, be it a primer, a guide, an orientative reference, an informative magazine, an orientative note, or any other document that has the objective of guiding the Administration in the abstract case.

It is important to note here that, in the case of advice-type consulting the responsibility for preparing the document lies with the audit team, unlike counsel-type work, where the responsibility for preparing the standard lies with management, with the audit team merely assisting the process.

Going back to the example of consulting related to risk management, an example of advice would be the development by the audit team of a guide on risk assessment, analysis and reporting for example.

The guide could contain, for example, the view of the standards and the main control bodies on the subject; the main errors in risk assessment, analysis, and reporting; the main models and examples of tools; or a step-by-step guide to effective risk assessment and reporting.

See that this is guidance in the abstract that applies to all risk management without getting involved in the concrete case.

To this end, advice-type consulting, we may use any of the techniques listed in item 7.1, or any other previously defined by the audit unit.

7.3 EXECUTION OF FACILITATION-TYPE CONSULTING

Facilitation-type consulting aims to facilitate a discussion process relevant to the organization, in a committee, in a commission, in a strategy meeting, or to facilitate the response to the organization's external control bodies.

Thus, when participating in a meeting, group, commission, or committee in which the advice of the CAE or any other staff member is used in the discussion process, we are faced with facilitating advice, *i.e.* in this case, the representative of the audit unit is "facilitating" the decision-making process through specific advice related to the topic of discussion.

Chart 24 - Flow of facilitation execution

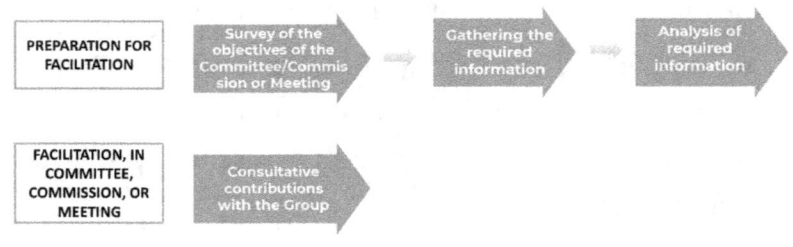

Source: Prepared by the author

The table above shows that the execution of facilitation is simpler than the other types of consulting, where it is necessary to first prepare for the consulting process and then offer the contribution in the most efficient way possible.

Advice offered in this type of consulting, as a rule, is recorded in meeting minutes, however, the results can be recorded in several other ways, such as the ones listed under counsel-type consulting.

You see, the basic difference between this type of work and the counsel type is that the latter is broader, while in a facilitation, the process is simpler and more direct, aiming to facilitate a discussion process in a meeting or in a committee/committee.

7.3.1 Meeting facilitation

The main challenge to be faced when facilitating in strategic meetings is the risk of losing the independence and objectivity of internal auditing due to the pressure that often exists for the audit to express itself in the concrete case.

In this case, in order to mitigate this risk, a technique I call risk-based advisory may be useful. This technique consists in raising risks and positive points of each possible decision.

Initially, a kind of *brainstorming* of the main risks involved in each possible decision is performed, and then the organization's main gains are identified, when deciding on one solution or another.

Therefore, in this case, for each possible decision a set of risks and positive points will be raised. This allows manager to make the decision based on relevant information regarding the process (risks and gains).

For auditors, the positive aspect of using this technique is that there is no advice as to which decision to take, but only a survey of the risks and positive points of the decision, and the manager is free to decide, by checking the risks involved in each of the options.

7.3.2 FACILITATION TO RESPOND TO EXTERNAL CONTROL BODIES

An example of this type of work is when the audit facilitates management's response to an inquiry from an external control body, such as a self-assessment of internal controls, or the organization's risk management, or any response in which the audit unit is facilitating management's work.

7.3.3 FACILITATION IN STRATEGIC COMMITTEES OR COMMISSIONS

Another typical example of facilitation-type consulting is the participation of auditors in committees and commissions where IA's participation is possible.

We remind you that the participation of audit representatives in specific and strategic committees and commissions is widely advised by good practices and *frameworks* related to internal audit.

However, some committees or commissions cannot have the participation of auditors, such as committees with the objective of determining responsibility (inquiries or Administrative Disciplinary Proceedings (PAD)) or whose objective is the administrative execution of procedures, such as the Permanent Bidding Commission or the Commission for Provisional or Definitive Receipt of Goods and Services procured.

Thus, to assess whether a specific committee is receptive to the participation of IA representatives, it is necessary to verify whether the group aims to provide advice that leads to the improvement of risk management, controls, and governance processes or whether it only aims to perform an act already previously defined, such as the examples specified above.

In order to support the auditor in the transmission of advice during facilitation-type consulting, any of the consulting techniques listed in the first item of this chapter may be used.

7.4 EXECUTION OF TRAINING-TYPE CONSULTING

Training-type consulting is the most easily perceived by those involved in the process. It occurs when participants of the internal audit unit act as instructors of a training activity.

This action can be in any modality (by remote teaching or in-person) and can be a formal action or merely a transfer of knowledge, as long as it takes place within the specific requirements of the consulting process.

To qualify as training-type consulting, the action must involve issues related to the organization's governance, risk management, or controls.

Another requirement mentioned before, which I think is relevant to remember, is that the transfer of knowledge is the responsibility of the auditing unit. If a given public officer, outside working hours, works as a paid or unpaid instructor in a training activity, we do not have training-type consulting. In this case, the auditor is a training service provider like any other

In order to qualify as training-type consulting, it must be an activity planned by internal audit, and not the exclusive initiative of a staff member acting outside audit responsibilities.

Therefore, the transfer of knowledge must occur within the consulting process as a product that makes up the provision of the service.

The table below shows a synthetic workflow of the training-type consulting.

Chart 25 - Training-type Consulting Workflow

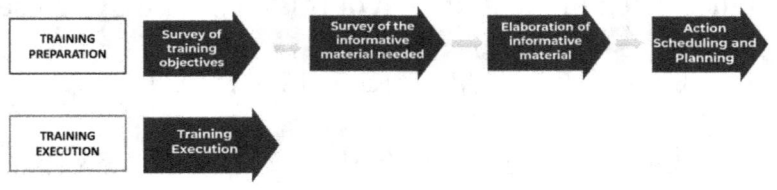

Source: Prepared by the author

As shown in the table above, the execution of training-type consulting is simple and consists in preparing for the transfer of knowledge and actually delivering the training.

CHAPTER 8

COMMUNICATING RESULTS

Communication of the results in consulting refers to the process of making the advice offered and the result of the work performed known to the *stakeholders*, that is, it is by means of this communication that the advice is formalized and disseminated to the requesting unit.

Initially, it is important to emphasize that the main purpose of the communication is to propose solutions in order to implement or improve the object of consulting.

Another relevant information, refers to the difference between an evaluation work report and a consulting work report.

In evaluation work, the report is the result of the work itself, since it contains the audit findings, conclusions, and the respective recommendations for necessary improvements. In consulting, the advice is given, as a rule, during the execution phase, when an Audit Note may be issued, minutes of meetings prepared, or other documents that deliver and forward the team's advice. In this way, the consulting report is not the result, because it is a document that reports the whole process developed and consolidates the information and the results already delivered, in a previous moment.

In other words, the proposals for solutions are made as the consulting progresses.

In our proposed example, still during execution, the team assists and proposes the standards to be used, assists in mapping the process, advises on the content of the policy and risk management manual drafts. And only at the end does it prepare a report recording everything that was produced in the executive phase of the activity.

Note that in this case the report will not be the result, it only records what has already been done during the execution of the work.

Of course there are exceptions, there may be report that is the result itself, but this is not the rule when it comes to consultative work.

If you are curious, look up consulting reports published by public sector audits and you will see that the report only records what has already been accomplished during the execution of the activity.

A relevant question to answer at this point is which document should be used to give advice during the consulting process?

To start answering the question we will evaluate the table below that describes the main steps of communicating results in consulting.

Chart 26- Communication of results

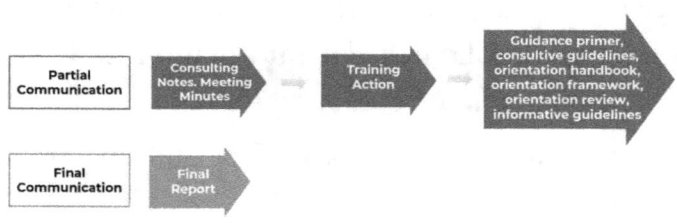

Source: Prepared by the author

By analyzing the table above, we see that the consulting process requires two forms of result communication: partial and final.

Partial communication is intended to provide advice while the work is still in progress. That is, before the consulting is finalized.

Answering the initial question, the truth is that, in consulting, there is a lot of freedom regarding the act used to formalize the counseling. It can be in a facilitation meeting where the counseling is recorded in meeting minutes. It can be a training session where the action itself is related to counseling. It can be an orientative document such as a guide, a primer, a guidance note. It could also be a consulting note or any equivalent document.

The main documents of partial communication used still in the execution phase of the work are:

1. consulting note;
2. meeting minutes;
3. training action; and
4. Guidance primer, consultive guidelines, orientation handbook, orientation framework, orientation review, informative guidelines.

8.1 Consulting Note

A Consulting note is the document used by the internal audit unit to communicate part of the result before the work is finalized. In other words, if there is a need to partially communicate the result, this should be done through an advisory note.

I particularly like to use the consulting note to report partial results. This is because, depending on the type of consulting, several products can be delivered through the NC and, in the end, the report issued will be merely informative, consolidating all information about the object analyzed, the products already delivered, and the results obtained.

So, going back to our consulting example, to advise regarding the risk management policy, an advisory note could be used containing whatever the audit deemed relevant to contain in the standard.

This note is usually used in counsel-type consulting, but it can be used in other types of work, such as advice, facilitation, and training. Due to its relevance, see this template for a consulting note.

Chart 27 - Consulting Note Template

CHAPTER 8 - COMMUNICATING RESULTS

CONSULTING NOTE

Internal Audit Department
2022 term

Introduction

Presentation of what the work is about, including its type, who requested and who approved the offer of consulting, preferably referencing the respective acts. You should specify the purpose of the consulting note, which is the motivation for the document.

Proposed Counseling

In this item you should propose the partial advice necessary to achieve the objective of the consulting. The presentation of the results must contain, at least: the situation encountered of the object, the possible solutions and the proposed advice.

Conclusion

The conclusion should be succinct, while portraying all relevant aspects of the work. Thus, the purpose of this item is to describe the problem presented, the proposed solutions, the main benefits achieved, and the synthesis of everything that is considered relevant and pertinent to the consulting service.

Consulting Team

list the members of the work team

Attachments

texts or documents created by third parties and used by the consulting team in composing the work. only attach if relevant to the understanding of the paper.

Appendices

texts or documents created by the consulting team itself, judged as relevant for understanding the work. you should only append if relevant to the understanding of the paper.

Source: Prepared by the author

8.2 Meeting Minutes

Meeting minutes are a brief document that records the relevant issues dealt with during the meeting held between the consulting unit and the audit unit providing the consulting service.

Thus, this document must contain the proposals, debates, deliberations, and decisions that took place at the meeting.

Communication through meeting minutes is typical of facilitation-type consulting work.

It is important that all meetings and interactions have some kind of record, and the minutes are an appropriate instrument for this. It is also important to register that the auditor is acting as a consultant, or providing consulting services.

8.3 Training Action

Training action is the form of communication of the results of training-type consulting.

This involves using the expertise and experience of the internal auditors to transfer knowledge to the organization's employees through training related to governance, risk management, and the institution's controls.

8.4 Guiding guide, advisory guidance, guiding primer, guiding reference, guiding magazine, and informative guidance.

These are examples of active guidance type consulting communication, where consulting is offered without necessarily having a management solution.

Explained: with the aim of guiding the organization, the IA unit - at its request, or on its own initiative - issues guidance by means of guides, guidance manuals, primers, informatives, advisory guidelines, or any other means that provides guidance in the abstract of any matter related to the organization's governance, risk management, and controls.

Examples of active guidance type consulting are: guidance manual on price research, primer - information security, quick reference guide - hiring IT solutions. [13]

It is worth noting that the above types of results communication are merely examples, and are not exhaustive.

As far as the final communication of the results is concerned, this occurs by means of the document called consulting report.

8.5 Consulting Report

Consultancy report is the classic way of communicating the results of the work. This type of document is used mainly in the course of counseling-type consulting but it can be used at the end of any consulting activity.

A good practice is to write a final consulting report to register the results of other types of work, such as advice, facilitation, and training, which have already been shown in other communications, such as Consultancy Notes, Meeting Minutes, Guidance Notes, and others.

With regard to facilitation-type consulting, this is work done throughout the year and that, due to its characteristics and specificities, does not always generate a final report for each facilitation work.

---

[13] Available at: http://www.stj.jus.br/sites/portalp/Institucional/auditoria-interna/Manuais-e-orientacoes.

For example, during facilitation in the risk management committee, in a controls self-assessment, or in the participation in strategic meetings, there may be no need to produce a report at the end of the work. However, it is relevant and recommended that, at the end of a period, at least annually, a report be prepared with the objective of registering the results of this work performed during the year.

This practice is interesting since many times the audit unit carries out several facilitation works, but does not register these results in the activity reports. In other words, it is work that is not accounted for by the audit

Thus, for example, at the end of a training activity, the audit unit can prepare a report with the objective of recording and communicating all the phases and the results of the work.

Or, at the end of a yearly term, a report can be prepared to register and communicate the results of the consulting work to stakeholders, such as facilitation, counseling, advice, or training, developed during that year.

Even in the case of the advisory consulting example where the products were delivered during its execution, at the end of the work, a report is required for the due record of the activities performed by the Audit.

A consulting report should be as succinct as possible, and preferably use resources such as graphs, tables, infographics, organizational charts, flow charts, maps, and any others that contribute to the clear and objective visualization of results.

The consulting report should portray at least the following topics:

1. Introduction
    1.1 presentation;
    1.2 objective;
    1.3 products;
    1.4 methodology;
    1.5 overview of the object;
    1.6 limitations and restrictions;
2. results obtained;
3. recommendations (if provided);
4. conclusion;
5. consulting team;
6. annexes and appendixes.

The above topics related to the introduction have already been studied in Chapter 6, which deals with planning, and should be adapted from the program detailed there for the consultant's report.

It is worth noting that the introduction should be succinct, preferably one or two paragraphs for each sub-item.

The remaining topics will be detailed below.

8.5.1 Results Obtained

This topic is responsible for effectively demonstrating the result of the work, portraying the advice proposed during the executive phase.

The topic "results" has the same purpose as the topic "audit findings" when carrying out evaluation work.

However, in consulting activities, there is not an audit finding, but one or more problems presented by the manager in order to obtain advice on possible solutions from the auditor.

Thus, the presentation of the results must contain, as a minimum: the situation found for the object, the possible solutions, and the proposed advice.

Situation Found

Situation found is the way the problem presented for the provision of the service is found, that is, it is the succinct and objective report of the current situation of the object consulted, before the implementation of the proposed solutions.

Possible solutions and proposed advice

Unlike an evaluation process in which the audit defines "what" should be done, in consulting work, the unit presents "how" it can be done, *i.e.* it helps the organization find a solution to the problem presented.

Therefore, this item of the report should specify the possible solutions found to the issue presented in the consultation and the advice proposed.

The audit unit may present more than one possible solution, and it is up to the manager to define the one that best meets the organization's needs.

It is common in a consulting process that, when the report is written, the solution has already been implemented during the execution of the work.

In this case, the audit unit will be able to report on the solutions presented and which were chosen and implemented to improve the object consulted.

8.5.2 Conclusion

The conclusion should be succinct, while bringing all relevant aspects of the work.

Thus, the purpose of this item is to describe the problem presented, the proposed solutions, the main benefits to be achieved, and a summary of everything that is deemed relevant and pertinent in providing consulting services.

The following is a sample Consultancy Report

Chart 28 - Consulting Report Template

Logo example
In horizontal format

CONSULTING REPORT

Internal Audit Department
2022 term

Executive Summary

Summary of the most important information from the paper, preferably in one page.

Summary

Introduction

a) Presentation of what the report is about, the type of work, who requested and who approved the offer of consultation, preferably referencing the respective acts;

b) Specify the objective of the activity that is nothing more than the reason for the requested work, it is what it is intended to achieve with the execution of the activity;

c) Products of the Consulting activities;

d) Methodology (how): the nature of the data examined should be registered (in summary form), the form of collection and treatment of such data, technical or legal references used as a basis for conducting the work, etc. If further detailing of the methodology employed is necessary, this should be done in the appendix (Detailing the Methodology);

e) Overview overview of the object: conceptualization of the object, functionality of the object, and how the object is found in the body;

f) Limitations/restrictions: this statement should only occur if there are limitations or restrictions to the work, such as, for example, the refusal of the manager to submit information or even its impossibility (example: document XX was not made available for analysis because it was going through the digitalization process);

Presented Results

This item must highlight the result of the work, proposing or portraying the appropriate solutions aimed at improving the organization's governance, risk management, and control processes;

The topic "results" has the same purpose as the topic "audit findings" when carrying out evaluation work;

However, in consulting activities, there is no audit finding, but rather one or more problems presented by the manager in order to obtain advice on possible solutions from the auditor;

Thus, the presentation of the results should contain, at a minimum: the situation found of the object, the possible solutions and the proposed advice.

Introductory paragraph (contextualization): the specific objective(s) of the work must be presented, and duly contextualized with synthetic information about the object analyzed, the risks, and the controls involved.

Results: Considering that the consulting report as a rule is not the result of the work, but contains the result that was developed during the execution of the activity, the products delivered by the consulting team or the proposed solutions aimed at meeting the objective of the work should be presented.

Recommendations

Initially it is worth pointing out that there will only be recommendations/advice when pertinent to the work and if previously agreed with the client unit. This is because the audit report may communicate results that have already been implemented with the help of the audit.

Thus, if the solution has already been implemented, a record is made of the advice and how it was adopted by the consulting unit, that is, how the implementation occurred during the consulting process.

Conclusion

The conclusion should be succinct, but also portray all relevant aspects of the work. Thus, the purpose of this item is to describe the problem presented, the proposed solutions, the main benefits achieved, and the synthesis of everything that is considered relevant and pertinent to the consulting service.

Consulting Team

Attachments

texts or documents created by third parties and used by the consulting team in composing the work. only attach if relevant to the understanding of the document.

Appendices

texts or documents created by the consulting team itself, judged as relevant for understanding the work. only append if relevant to the understanding of the document.

CHAPTER 9

MONITORING AND EVALUATION

IPPF Standard 2500.C1 establishes that the internal audit activity shall monitor the disposition of the results of consulting work to the extent previously agreed upon with the client. This means that the monitoring of consulting results must comply with the agreement made with the consulting unit.

It is worth remembering that the agreement regarding roles and responsibilities within a consulting process (which includes monitoring) is registered in the consulting program.

Thus, this document must register whether or not the results will be subject to monitoring and, if so, the extent and frequency of this process.

The extent of consulting refers to the form and scope agreed upon with the requesting manager.

In this respect, criteria such as: will all advisories be monitored or only the most relevant ones? Will it be checked only if Management has implemented the advice or will the quality and outcome of the implementation be evaluated? Will it be possible or not to issue new advice during monitoring?

Regarding the periodicity, the agreement must foresee how long after the work is done the monitoring will take place, and for how long the consulting process will be monitored.

It should be noted that in consulting services, unlike assessment work, no recommendations are issued, but rather advice regarding possible solutions related to governance, risk management, and the organization's controls.

Thus, there is no obligation to monitor the results, which will only be done if previously agreed with the consulting unit.

Although it is not mandatory to monitor the consulting work, it is important to adopt some kind of monitoring of the consulting implementation for the purposes of accounting for benefits, whether financial or non-financial.

With regard to quality assessment, IPPF Standard 1300 specifies that the head of the internal audit unit should develop and maintain a quality assurance and improvement program that encompasses all aspects of the internal audit activity.

Thus, all audit activities must undergo an evaluation process.

Since consulting is an important internal auditing activity, it must also undergo a continuous evaluation process.

Therefore, all consulting work must undergo an evaluation process, which includes, at a minimum:

- the consulting team;
- the consultant's supervisor; and
- the consulting unit.

The objective of this evaluation is to provide *feedback* to the audit unit, in order to offer a diagnosis of the quality of the work offered and developed, in addition to adopting the necessary measures to improve the activity.

CHAPTER 10

THE PROCESS OF CHANGE

If you, the reader, have come this far, it is likely that you have come to the conclusion of the need for personal and institutional change in your auditing unit, and it is even likely that you are thinking right now: "Wow, this book changed my way of 'seeing' consulting".

However, my big goal with this book is not to change the way you see consulting, but rather to change the way you "live" consulting, practice it, execute it, make a difference.

However, I have some not very pleasant news: few people will actually put what they learn here into practice, and do you know why? Because it requires change, and change is hard, because it requires will and dedication, it is a lot of work.

Change is a process much more related to deconstruction than to construction.

In order to change, you must initially "learn to unlearn", so that you can then build the new, reinvent that which will take you to the next level.

Our mind is an incredible machine that plays a crucial role in our survival and perpetuation of the species.

It strives to protect us, and this protection is expressed in avoiding everything that seems to represent some danger, some abnormality, some change.

At first glance, this seems very good, very appropriate to the reality we live in today and to the reality our ancestors lived in, but this is only true if our need is just to stay alive, and you know very well that this does not meet the desires of contemporary society.

We need more, much more than just survival.

Changing is a process that requires effort to convince our mind that we do not need protection in that matter.

To put this in context, I'll tell you a story.

I am from Minas Gerais State, but I have been living in Brasília for over 20 years. My mother often comes to visit me. And in this period we always go to a religious celebration that takes place on Sunday night.

Once, I realized that my mother always sat on the same pew, in the same place. So, once, I told her:

- Mom, let's sit on the other side, on another pew.

She had a wary expression on her face, but changed places anyway, not to displease me.

There, at that moment, we greeted other people, sat down and waited for the celebration to begin. At that moment I realized that my mother had a "frown" on her face.

Have you ever seen a "grumpy" person from Minas Gerais? So I asked her what was going on, and she said:

- Son, I don't like to change places. Back home I have been going to church for more than 20 years and I always sit in the same pew. Now you come and force me to change.

- Mom, have you noticed that here, in this place, we greet different people?

CHAPTER 10 - THE PROCESS OF CHANGE

- Yes, I got it. - She replied.

- You see that here you have a better view because we are closer to the stage? - I continued.

- Yes, I do. - she said.

- Can you see that the sound is better here because there is a speaker nearby? - I asked, to which she replied in the affirmative.

- So, Mom, change is something positive, you have changed and improved the view, the sound, the people, the air-conditioning... you see that change is good?

- It's true, son, I really need to learn to change.

- Mom, do you work in Minas Gerais? - I asked, taking advantage of the cue. As if I didn't know!

- I work, yes, my son.

- And how long have you been working there?

- 12 years old.

- And do you enjoy your work?

- God forbid! I don't like "this", "that", "that" and "that other".

A few minutes later, when she finished the whole rant, I said:

- Isn't it time for you to sit on another pew in life as well?

She thoughtfully, and disappointed in herself, replied:

- It is true, my son, I really need to change some things.

And my little mother, over 60 years old, is learning to sit in another pew in church and in life.

Just like my mother, we need to learn to change, we need to get up, from what I call, the "oh no seat".

Do you know the oh no seat?

It's like: "oh-no, consulting is too hard! Oh-no, that doesn't work in my institution! Oh-no, managers don't want to know about it! Oh-no, it has always been like that, why change? Oh-no! Oh no!"

We need to learn to get up from the "oh-no seat" and sit with those who make a difference, with those who not only change, but are channels of change wherever they go.

So I invite you to believe.

To believe that we have the power to change things, to make a difference, to add value, to truly contribute with our work to the society we live in.

So create opportunities, accept challenges, learn, unlearn, and learn again!

Make it happen, make a difference, make it *different*!

Make it worthwhile!

Big hugs and much success to all!

REFERENCES

ASSOCIAÇÃO BRASILEIRA DE NORMAS TÉCNICAS (ABNT). *ISO NBR 31000*: gestão de riscos – princípios e diretrizes. Rio de Janeiro: ABNT, 2009.

BRASIL. Conselho Nacional de Justiça (CNJ). *Resolução CNJ nº 308*, de 11 de março de 2020a. Organiza as atividades de auditoria interna do Poder Judiciário, sob a forma de sistema, e cria a Comissão Permanente de Auditoria. Disponível em: https://atos.cnj.jus.br/atos/detalhar/3288. Acesso em: 4 out. 2020.

BRASIL. Conselho Nacional de Justiça (CNJ). *Resolução CNJ nº 309*, de 11 de março de 2020b. Aprova as Diretrizes Técnicas das Atividades de Auditoria Interna Governamental do Poder Judiciário (DiraudJud) e dá outras providências. Disponível em: https://atos.cnj.jus.br/atos/detalhar/3289. Acesso em: 4 out. 2020.

BRASIL. Controladoria-Geral da União. Ministério da Justiça e Segurança Pública. *Relatório de Consultoria*. Prestação de serviço de consultoria voltado para processos de governança, gerenciamento de riscos e controles internos. Brasília, DF: Poder Executivo, 2019.

BRASIL. Decreto nº 9.203, de 23 de novembro de 2017: dispõe sobre a política de governança da administração pública federal direta, autárquica e fundacional. *Diário Oficial da União*: Brasília, DF, 2017a. Disponível em: http://www.planalto.gov.br/ccivil_03/_Ato2015-2018/2017/Decreto/D9203.htm. Acesso em: 21 ago. 2020.

BRASIL. *Instrução Normativa nº 3*, de 9 de junho de 2017b. Aprova o Referencial Técnico da Auditoria Interna Governamental do Poder Executivo Federal. Disponível em: https://www.in.gov.br/materia//asset_publisher/KujrwoTZC2Mb/content/id/19111706/do1-2017-06-12-instrucao-normativa-n-3-de-9-de-junho-de-2017-19111304. Acesso em: 4 out. 2020.

BRASIL. *Instrução Normativa SFC nº 8*, de 6 de dezembro de 2017c. Aprova o Manual de Orientações Técnicas da Atividade de Auditoria Interna Governamental do Poder Executivo Federal. Disponível em: https://

www.in.gov.br/materia/-/asset_publisher/KujrwoTZC2Mb/content/id/869942/do1-2017-12-08-instrucao-normativa-n-8-de-6-de-dezembro-de-2017-869938. Acesso em: 4 out. 2020.

BRASIL. Lei nº 14.133, de 1º de abril de 2021. Lei de Licitações e Contratos Administrativos. *Diário Oficial da União*: Brasília, DF, 2021. Disponível em: http://www.planalto.gov.br/ccivil_03/_ato2019-2022/2021 /lei/L14133.htm. Acesso em: 08 abr. 2021.

INSTITUTO DE AUDITORES INTERNOS DO BRASIL. *Declaração de posicionamento do IIA*: as Três Linhas de Defesa no Gerenciamento Eficaz de Riscos e Controles. Altamonte

Springs: IIA Brasil, 2009. Disponível em: https://iiabrasil.org.br/korbilload/upl/ippf/downloads/declarao-de-pos-ippf-00000001-21052018101250.pdf. Acesso em: 12 abr. 2020.

INSTITUTO DE AUDITORES INTERNOS DO BRASIL. *Estrutura Internacional de Práticas Profissionais (International Professional Practices Framework* – IPPF). Normas Internacionais para a Prática Profissional de Auditoria Interna. Altamonte

Springs: IIA Brasil, [2020]. Disponível em: https://iiabrasil.org.br//ippf/introducao-as-normas. Acesso em: 7 abr. 2020.

INSTITUTO DE AUDITORES INTERNOS DO BRASIL (IIA BRASIL). *Normas Internacionais para a prática de Auditoria Interna (Normas)*. Altamonte Springs: IIA Brasil, 2017. Disponível em: https://iiabrasil.org.br/korbilload/upl/ippf/downloads/normasinternaci-ippf-00000001-02042018191815.pdf. Acesso em: 12 abr. 2020.

ORGANIZAÇÃO INTERNACIONAL DAS ENTIDADES FISCALIZADORAS SUPERIORES – INTOSAI. *Estrutura de Pronunciamentos Profissionais da INTOSAI*, [2021]. Disponível em: https://www.issai.org/. Acesso em: 3 jun. 2021.

TRIBUNAL DE CONTAS DO ESTADO DA BAHIA. *Normas de Auditoria Governamental (NAGs) aplicáveis ao controle externo*. Salvador: TCE-BA, 2007.

TRIBUNAL DE CONTAS DA UNIÃO. *Acórdão Plenário– TCU nº 814*, de 18 de abril de 2018. Fiscalização realizada em cumprimento aos acórdãos 3.608/2014, 1.273/2015 e 1.171/2017, todos do plenário. Oportunidades de melhoria no processo de convergência dos procedimentos das unidades de controle interno do poder legislativo federal e do tribunal de contas da união às normas internacionais de auditoria interna. Competência e capacidade das unidades de controle interno em realizar auditorias financeiras, em apoio à missão constitucional do TCU. Disponível em: https://pesquisa.apps.tcu. gov.br/#/documento/acordao– completo/*/NUMACORDAO3A81420A-NOACORDAO3A201820COLEGIADO3A22PlenC3A1rio22/DTRELEVAN-CIA2odesc2C20NUMACORDAOINT2odesc/0/20?uuid=6527fc10– 067d– 11eb– 8f07– 55fa1d65d3fe. Acesso em: 4 out. 2020.

TRIBUNAL DE CONTAS DA UNIÃO. *Acórdão TCU – Plenário nº 1.074*, de 20 de maio de 2009. Trata-se de levantamento (de natureza operacional) realizado como parte dos trabalhos do Tema de Maior Significância (TMS) n. 9 – Governança no Setor Público –, em conformidade com o Plano de Fiscalização 2008/2009 aprovado pelo Plenário do TCU (Ata n. 09, de 26/3/2008). Disponível em: https://pesquisa.apps.tcu.gov.br/#/documento/acordao-completo/*/NUMACORDAOA107420ANOACORDAO-A200920COLEGIADOAPlenCA1rio/DTRELEVANCIAdesCNUMACOR-DAOINTdesc/?uuid=6527fc10-067d-11eb-8f07-55fa1d65d3fe. Acesso em: 4 out. 2020.

TRIBUNAL DE CONTAS DA UNIÃO. *Acórdão TCU – Plenário nº 1.171*, de 7 de junho de 2017. Trata- se de Fiscalização, na modalidade Levantamento, aprovada pelas Portarias de Fiscalização 383/16 (peça 1) e 697/16 (peça 6), Fiscalis 172/2016, decorrente da deliberação do Acórdão 1.273/2015 – TCU – Plenário (TC 020.830/2014– 9), que tratou da situação da governança pública em âmbito nacional do panorama da governança e gestão das aquisições em âmbito estadual, distrital e municipal; e do Acórdão 3.608/2014 – TCU – Plenário (TC 016.937/2012– 0), que materializou a proposta de estratégia de fortalecimento da auditoria financeira no TCU. Disponível em: https://pesquisa.apps.tcu.gov.br/#/documento/acordao– completo/*/ NUMACORDAOA117120ANOACORDAOA201720COLEGIADOAPlen-CA1rio/DTRELEVANCIAdescCNUMACORDAOINTdesc/?uuid=6527fc-10-067d-11eb-8f0755fa1d65d3fe. Acesso em: 4 out. 2020.

TRIBUNAL DE CONTAS DA UNIÃO. *Acórdão TCU – Plenário nº 1.745/2020 – Plenário*, de 8 de julho de 2020. Fiscalização realizada em cumprimento aos acórdãos 3.608/2014 e 1.273/2015. Ambos do plenário. Oportunidades de melhoria no processo de convergência dos procedimentos das unidades de controle interno do poder judiciário às normas internacionais de auditoria interna. Disponível em: https://pesquisa.apps.tcu.gov.br/#/documento/acordao- completo/*/NUMACORDAO%253A1745%2520ANOACORDAO%253A2020%2520COLEGIADO%253A%2522Plen%25C3%25A1rio%2522/DTRELEVANCIA%2520desc%252C%2520NUMACORDAOINT%2520desc/0/%2520?uuid=6527fc10-067d-11eb-8f07-55fa1d65d3fe. Acesso em: 4 out. 2020.

TRIBUNAL DE CONTAS DA UNIÃO. *Acórdão Plenário – TCU nº 2.622*, de 21 de outubro de 2015. Levantamento. Governança e gestão das aquisições na administração pública federal. Análise sistêmica das oportunidades de melhoria. Disponível em: https://pesquisa.apps.tcu.gov.br/#/documento/acordao- completo/*/NUMACORDAO%253A2622%2520ANOACORDAO%253A2015%2520COLEGIADO%253A%2522Plen%25C3%25A1rio%2522/DTRELEVANCIA%2520desc%252C%2520NUMACORDAOINT%2520desc/0/%2520?uuid=e93d35c0-7d06-11ea-9bea-0f4b85a43f45. Acesso em: 12 abr. 2020.

TRIBUNAL DE CONTAS DA UNIÃO. *Glossário de termos do controle externo*, 1 set. 2012. Disponível em: https://portal.tcu.gov.br/biblioteca-digital/glossario-de-termos-do-controle-externo.htm. Acesso em: 6 jun. 2020.

TRIBUNAL DE CONTAS DA UNIÃO. *Normas de Auditoria do Tribunal de Contas da União (NAT)*. Legislação e normativos, 5 nov. 2011. Disponível em: https://portal.tcu.gov.br/biblioteca-digital/normas-de-auditoria-do-tribunal-de-contas-da-uniao-nat.htm. Acesso em: 4 out. 2020.

TRIBUNAL DE CONTAS DA UNIÃO. Avaliação dos Controles Internos. Disponível em< https://portal.tcu.gov.br/biblioteca-digital/avaliacao-de-controles-internos-8A81881E747486F301749B74F46749F7.htm>. Acesso em 10 set 2022

DAYCHOUM, Merhi. 40 Ferramentas e técnicas de gerenciamento. Rio de Janeiro: Brasport, 2007

RICHARD A. KRUGER, Mary Anne Casey .Focus Groups: A Practical Guide for Applied Research . California.Sage, 2000.

MORGAN, G. Imagens da organização. 1.ed. São Paulo: Atlas, 1996

COHEN, Ernesto; MARTINEZ, Rodrigo. Manual de formulacion, evaluacion y monitoreo de proyectos sociales. División de Desarrollo Social. Comisión Económica para América Latina (CEPAL), 2004. Disponível em< https://dds.cepal.org/redesoc/archivos_recursos/242/Manual_dds_200408.pdf>. Acesso em 10 set 2022.

Annette Schandl MSIB, Philip L. Foster. COSO Internal Control (The Comitee of Sponsoring Organizations) – Integrated Framework: An Implementation Guide for the Healthcare Provider Industry |.Coso .org.2019. Disponível em;< https://www.coso.org/Shared%20Documents/CROWE-COSO-Internal-Control-Integrated-Framework.pdf> Acesso em 10 set 2022

TRIBUNAL DE CONTAS DA UNIÃO. Glossário dos Termos do Controle Externo. Disponível em: <<https://portal.tcu.gov.br/biblioteca-digital/glossario-de-termos-do-controle-externo.htm>. Acesso em: 10 set. 2022

TRIBUNAL DE CONTAS DA UNIÃO. Técnicas de Entrevista para Auditorias. Disponível em: < https://portal.tcu.gov.br/lumis/portal/file/fileDownload.jsp?fileId=8A8182A258FE9A84015903D992B9083A> Acesso em: 10 set. 2022

GOVERNMENT AUDIT CONSULTING

APPENDIX A

CONSULTING PROCESS WORKFLOWS

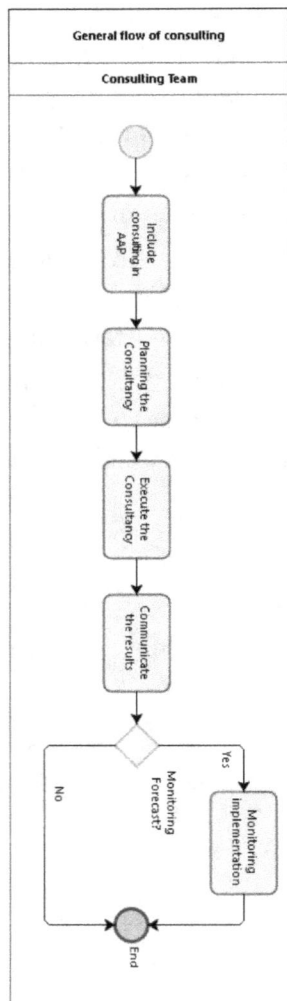

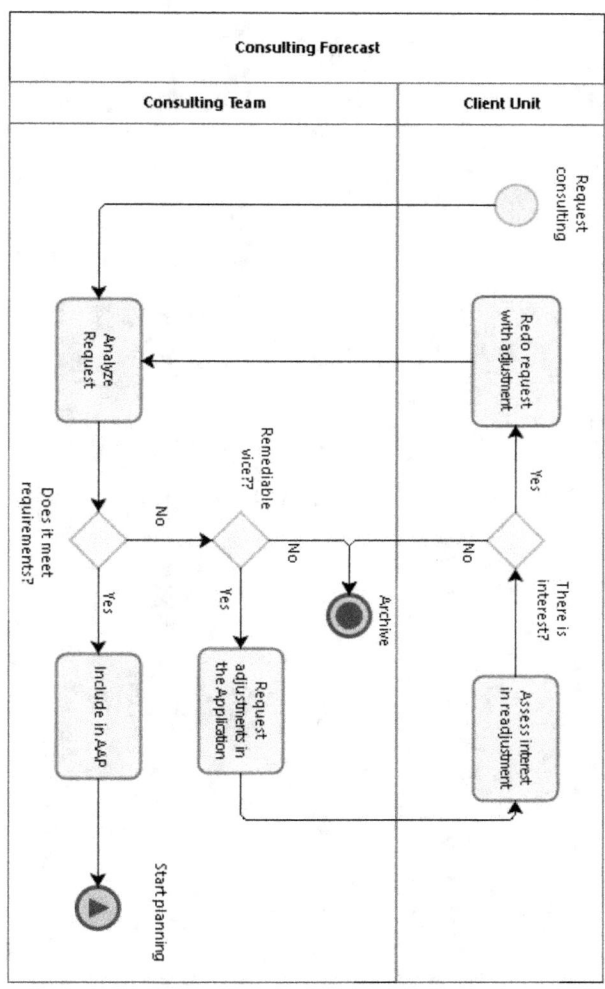

GOVERNMENT AUDIT CONSULTING

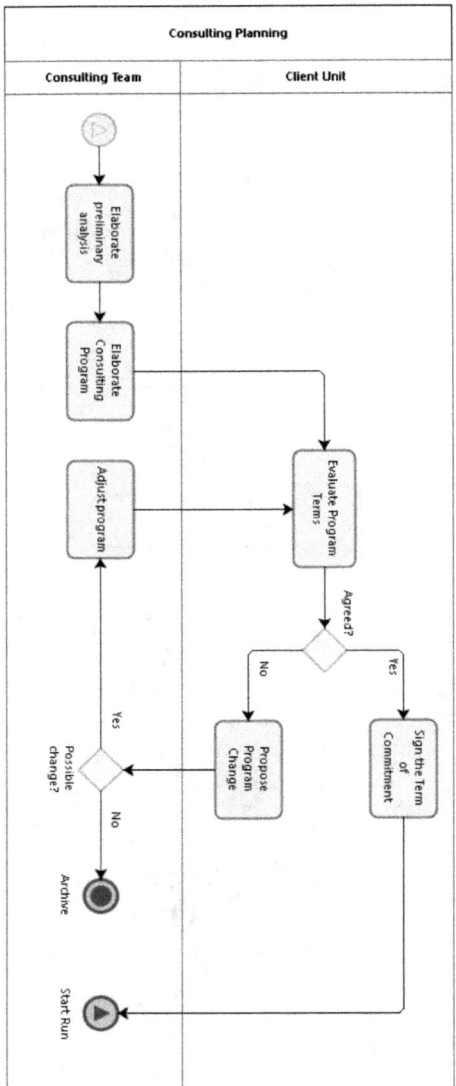

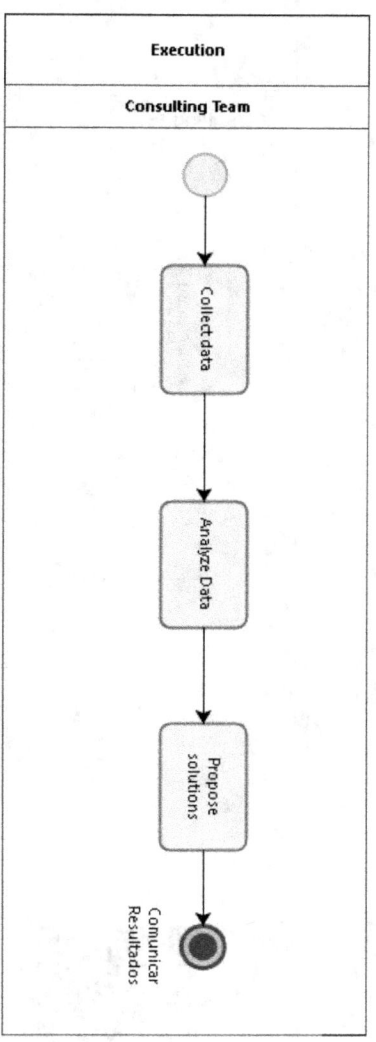

GOVERNMENT AUDIT CONSULTING

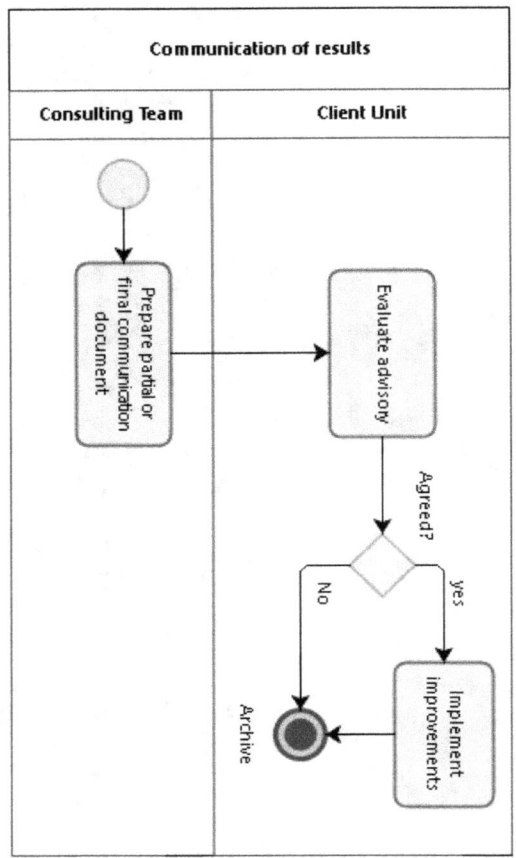

212

Appendix B

SURVEY WITH KEY *STAKEHOLDERS*

This research aimed to capture and learn about the real perception of these different actors regarding the elaboration and execution of consulting work by the Internal Audit (IA) units of the Brazilian government.

To analyze and understand the results found, it should be mentioned that questionnaires were sent to approximately 200 departments of the three branches of power (Executive, Legislative, and Judiciary), and responses were obtained from 468 auditors and managers from 133 different public institutions.

For a better understanding and analysis of the conclusions pointed out below, the results will be presented according to the following criteria: first, information regarding the respondents' profiles; then, their perspective on the possibility of consulting work; and, finally, the understanding of control bodies and other institutions that research or regulate the subject.

1.1 Consulting in the view of the government internal auditor

1.1.1 Auditor profile

With regard to the profile of the auditors, the questionnaires were answered by professionals who fit into the following groups: preponderant age bracket above 45 years, majority male, more than 5 years of experience in auditing, and higher education level.

It can also be seen that only 5% of the respondents stated that their department or governmental body had a specific auditor position or career path.

1.1.2 NAMES OF THE UNITS

The first relevant question in the survey refers to the denomination of the units responsible for the audit work. As shown in the table below, about 43% of the units are called "Internal Control", and not Internal Audit, the format recommended by the Standards and the main control bodies.

In this author's understanding, this approach is relevant, as it is assumed that the denomination "Internal Control" can interfere in the auditors' perception, since, in general, this denomination creates confusion - especially on the part of the Admiistration - in relation to the division of competencies between audited and auditing units.

A large portion of the managers understands that "internal controls" are an exclusive attribution of the "Internal Control Unit".

This misperception negatively impacts the managers' assessment of consulting.

In the same sense, the existence of a specific auditor position or career path (mentioned in the previous item) indicates that the responsibilities are apparently better defined among the units, increasing the audited unit's perception of the roles of each one within the organization.

Table 1 - Internal Audit × Internal Control

ISSUES	YES	NO
Is the unit in which you perform your activities called Internal Audit?	243	184
Does your organization have its own auditor career path?	23	404

Source: Prepared by the author.

According to the content of Table 1, it can be seen that the percentage of units called "Internal Audit" among those consulted is the majority, representing 56% of all those consulted.

On the other hand, the number of units that have developed their own career path is low, as indicated by only 5% of the respondents.

In this book, the term *Internal Audit* is adopted.

1.1.3 POSITIONING IN RELATION TO CONSULTING WORK

The following table contains the position of the auditors regarding the performance of consulting work by Internal Audit.

Table 2 - Auditors' evaluation

ISSUES	YES	NO
In your opinion, would the managers of your organization like to receive consulting work offered by the internal audit or internal control unit?	374	53
In your organization, does the internal audit or internal control unit perform consulting work?	245	182

If your internal audit or internal control unit does not yet perform consulting services, do you intend to do so in the next few years?	82	9
Do you consider yourself able to perform consulting services?	210	217
Do you believe that the internal audit or internal control unit adds value by doing consulting work?	378	49
In your opinion, should the internal audit or internal control unit perform consulting work?	352	75
Do you believe that the internal audit or internal control unit loses its independence when performing consulting services?	88	339

Source: Prepared by the author.

From the analysis of the above information, it was found that 88% of the surveyed auditors believe that the managers of their organization would like to receive consulting work offered by the internal audit unit.

Another relevant piece of information is that, of all the people interviewed, approximately 57% said that their units already perform consulting work, and only 2% said that their units do not intend to do consulting work in the next few years.

Another point worth mentioning is that more than half of the respondents (51%) stated that they did not feel prepared to perform consulting activities. Among the reasons alleged for the lack of aptitude were: lack of training (35%), lack of guidelines (26%), absence of guides and manuals (32%), and others

(26%).

For 82% of the professionals, the internal audit or internal control unit should perform consulting work. On the other hand, for the 18% who answered it should not, 39% cited as justification for their rejection that there would be a loss of independence; 30%, that it is not the auditing business; 12% claimed lack of knowledge; and 18%, other reasons.

The result of this part of the survey motivated me even more to write this book, because, if only 2% of the respondents stated that their units do not intend to develop consulting activities in the next few years, and if more than half of the respondents do not consider themselves apt to develop this type of activity, it is necessary to provide these professionals with relevant information that can help them to adequately use this important tool for IA.

In the survey, the questions had an exploratory nature, since they allowed the auditor to express his opinion freely in relation to what was understood as consulting.

Some of the statements received in the questionnaire are transcribed below. It is worth pointing out that the survey focused on collecting the opinion of the *stakeholders*, which is why there will be no mention of the statements' authors.

1. In my view, audit consulting is very appropriate depending on the organizational context, and the opposite is true. In other words, an institution with a mature organizational history, robust technical level, and an advanced structure, can dispense, to some extent, with the most basic audit work. On the other hand, another organization with different characteristics from that one would already need this type of service to a great extent.

2. [Consulting is the] Best way for Auditing to add value and strengthen its relationship with the audited unit.

3. Consulting is a typical activity of internal auditing which, in the public sector, is very incipient. For a long time, all the efforts of the "Internal Control" were directed to seek independence from the manager, and because of this, a mentality of distancing auditors from the Administration was wrongly created. Therefore, the implementation of this activity requires a strong awareness and acculturation campaign.

4. I think it is going to be a trend in Public Administration. I think it will prevent many problems, such as rework, waste of material, slowness in accomplishing tasks, and excessive bureaucratization.

5. It is a new aspect of work that auditing will have to perfect because it will bring more effective results for the Administration.

6. In my perception, audit consulting is one of the main ways to add value to the institution.

7. It seems clear to me that consulting is part of a set of transformations that have been taking place in Public Administration, in Corporate Management, and in the consciousness of the world as a whole, in which more and more things will be integrated and shared, especially in the concept and context of governance and management.

8. I believe that consulting will strengthen and enhance the auditor's role even more and will create a good opportunity to increase this field of activity.

See what important contributions can be identified from the analysis of colleagues' manifestations regarding audit consulting.

1.2 Consulting in the view of client managers

The following table shows the perspective of the managers of public institutions regarding the provision of consulting services by internal auditing:

Chart 3 - Managers' evaluation (direct clients)

ISSUES	YES	NO
Are you aware that, besides the evaluation process, the audit or internal control unit can also perform consulting work in the risk management, governance and control processes?	30	11
In your opinion, should the audit or internal control unit perform consulting work?	39	2
Do you believe that the audit or internal control unit adds value by doing consulting work?	38	3
In your opinion, are the audit or internal control units able to perform consulting work?	31	10
Would you like to receive consulting services from the audit or internal control unit, aimed at improving your work processes related to governance, risk management, and internal controls?	34	7

Source: Prepared by the author.

The data in Chart 3 show that about 27% of the managers interviewed are unaware that the internal audit unit can offer services of a consultative nature.

Relevant data in the table is that, for 95% of the respondents, the audit unit should develop consulting work. And, for 93% of them, the audit unit adds value by doing this kind of work.

The vast majority of the managers interviewed (83%) stated that they would like to receive consulting services from the audit unit, with a view to improving their work processes related to governance, risk management, and internal controls.

Finally, about 76% of them responded that they believe that the audit units are able to perform consulting work.

For those who responded that they believe the audit units are not prepared to offer consulting work, the main arguments were: lack of experience, lack of knowledge regarding business rules, and lack of technical training.

Note that the managers have a higher awareness than the auditors regarding the preparation of the team to perform consulting work, since less than 50% of the auditing professionals consider themselves prepared for such a task, and about 76% of the managers consider them prepared for the activity.

1.3 CONSULTING IN THE VIEW OF LEADERS OF THE MAIN INSTITUTIONS THAT BRING TOGETHER PROFESSIONALS IN THE AREA OF AUDIT AND CONTROL

With the objective of obtaining the position of the main professional congregation bodies in the area of auditing and control of the public administration, the understanding of the leaders of the National Council for Internal Control (CONACI), of the Federal Council of Directors of Internal Control Bodies (DICON), and of the Institute of Internal Auditors (IIA) was collected.

The leaders of the researched institutions have very similar positions in relation to the consulting activity. Thus, I will summarize the statements of each of the representatives mentioned.

Geovani Ferreira de Oliveira, federal auditor of external control, president of the DICON Council in the biennium 2016/2018:

> *By playing the role of consultant, internal auditing positions itself as an important partner in the management of organizations, which helps to dispel the police-like and punitive image that it has carried over the decades and that, fortunately, has been changing in recent times. The internal audit is part of the organization and should, within its specialties and from the height of its preparation, help the organization to which it belongs to achieve its most relevant objectives.*

Paulo Gomes - General Manager of IIA Brazil and Cristiane Casagrande - General Manager of the same Institute:

> *Internal Auditing aims to add value to organizations, contributing to the improvement of processes to achieve goals and helping High Administration and/or the board in their decision making. Consulting work has been guiding a new preventative view within the Internal Audit activities so that recommendations precede the occurrence of the problem.*
>
> *It is worth noting that the consulting activity must be previously evaluated by the head of internal auditing, in order to identify restrictions that harm his independence in performing the work, as well as to be aware that the auditors involved in the work must abstain from assuming any management responsibilities.*
>
> *With due care, it is extremely healthy to use this new concept within internal auditing activities.*

Finally, according to Leonardo de Araújo Ferraz, president of CONACI:

> *It is well known that, on a theoretical and conceptual level, there is relative consensus that both evaluation and consulting fall within the delimitation of the activities related to the (macro) function of Auditing within the scope of the unit responsible for Internal Control.*

Thus, it can be seen that the opinion of the leaders of the bodies consulted is in line with the understanding of the auditors and of the managers who are clients of the consulting process in the sense of recognizing the importance of the consulting activity for the improvement of governance processes, risk management, and organizational controls.

1.4 Consulting in the View of the Main Control Bodies and Other Institutes

The following are the views of the various control bodies on audit consulting, as well as citing the international Standards that deal with the subject.

Federal Court of Accounts (TCU)

In a number of cases the Federal Court of Accounts (TCU) has emphasized the importance of consulting work conducted by the various internal audit units of the Brazilian government.

Examples of Decisions containing recommendations on the subject are:

- Court Decision no. 1.074/2009 - Plenary;
- Court Decision no. 1,171/2017 - Plenary;
- Court Decision no. 814/2018 - Plenary;
- Court Decision no. 1.745/2020 - Plenary.

Through Court Decision no. 814/2018 - Plenary, the Federal Court of Accounts (TCU) recommended the Internal Control Secretariat of the Federal Senate to evaluate the convenience and opportunity to include, in its next annual audit plans, the performance of typical consulting activities.

In a decision TCU Court Decision no. 1745/2020 - Plenary, the Court of Accounts recommended that the internal audit of the Supreme Federal Court prepare and publish a Consulting Manual to guide the execution of internal audit activity in alignment with IPPF 2040.[14]

Office of the Comptroller General (CGU)

In recent years, the Office of the Comptroller General has standardized and executed relevant consulting work.

Through the Technical Guidelines for Government Internal Audit Activity - established through Normative Instruction No. 3, of June 9, 2017 - the Office regulated the provision of consulting services by internal audits in the Federal Executive Branch.

Through SFC Normative Instruction No. 8 of December 6, 2017, the Office instituted the Manual of Technical Guidelines for Government Internal Audit Activity of the Federal Executive, including the procedures to be adopted when providing services of an advisory nature.

Among the Office's activities, one example is the consulting service for the National Public Security and Social Defense Policy (PNSPDS) and the National Public Security Plan (PNSP).[15]

---

[14] The chief audit executive should establish policy and procedures to guide internal audit activity.
[15] Consulting report available at https://auditoria.cgu.gov.br/download/13440.pdf.

National Justice Council (CNJ)

The National Justice Council, through CNJ no. Resolution 309/2020, which approved the Technical Guidelines for the Government Internal Auditing Activities in the Judiciary, regulated the provision of advisory services by the internal audits of the Judiciary.

Consulting is also referenced as a typical internal audit activity in CNJ Resolution 308/2020, which organized the internal audit activities of the Judiciary in the form of a System and created the Permanent Audit Committee.

GOVERNMENT AUDIT CONSULTING

Glossário Português-Inglês

Português	Inglês
Ação de Capacitação	Training Action
AI: Auditoria Interna	IA: Internal Audit
Análise RECI (Responsável, executado, consultado e informado)	RACI Analysis (Responsible, accountable, consulted, and informed)
Assessoramento	Counsel
Ata de Reunião	Meeting Minutes
CEA: Chefe Executivo de Auditoria	CAE: Chief Audit Executive
CGU: Controladoria-Geral da União	Office of the Comptroller General (CGU)
CJF: Conselho da Justiça Federal	Council of Federal Justice (CJF)
CNJ: Conselho Nacional de Justiça	National Justice Council (CNJ)
CONACI: Conselho Nacional de Controle Interno	National Council for Internal Control (CONACI)
CSJT: Conselho Superior da Justiça do Trabalho	Superior Labor Justice Council (CSJT)
DICON: Conselho de Dirigentes de Órgãos de Controle Interno da União	Federal Council of Directors of Internal Control Bodies (DICON)
Facilitação	Facilitation
Guia orientativo, orientação consultiva, cartilha orientativa, referencial orientativo, revista orientativa e orientação informativa	Guidance primer, consultive guidelines, orientation handbook, orientation framework, orientation review, informative guidelines
IIA: Instituto de Auditores Internos	IIA: Institute of Internal Auditors

IPPFs: Normas Internacionais para a Prática Profissional de Auditoria Interna.	IPPFs: International Standards for the Professional Practice of Internal Auditing
NAG: Normas de Auditora Governamental	NAG: Government Auditing Standards
NAT: Normas de Auditoria do Tribunal de Contas da União	NAT: Auditing Standards of the Federal Court of Accounts
Nota de Consultoria	Consulting Note
Orientação	Advice
PAA: Plano de Auditoria Anual	Annual Audit Plan (AAP)
PAD: Procedimento Administrativo Disciplinar	Administrative Disciplinary Proceedings (PAD)
Referencial Técnico da Atividade de Auditoria Interna Governamental do Poder Executivo Federal	Technical Guidelines for the Government Internal Auditing Activity of the Federal Executive Branch
Relatório de Consultoria	Consulting Report
TCU: Tribunal de Contas da União	Federal Court of Accounts (TCU)
Termo de Compromisso	Term of Commitment
Treinamento	Training

www.ingramcontent.com/pod-product-compliance
Lightning Source LLC
Chambersburg PA
CBHW052347220526
45465CB00003BA/1002